WIRED
FOR
BRILLIANCE

A Parent's Guide to Nurturing **ADHD** Minds

SAKINA KAGALWALA

ISBN
Paperback: 979-8-89233-850-9
Hardcase: 979-8-89233-902-5

Contents

Acknowledgment

To my wonderful children,

To my son, who, with his boundless energy and unique perspective, taught me the true meaning of parenting. Your ADHD journey has been a transformative experience, leading me to discover new dimensions of love, patience, and understanding. Your vibrant spirit has illuminated the path to a more compassionate and inclusive form of parenting, one that celebrates differences and cherishes every moment.

To my daughter, a steadfast pillar of strength and unwavering support throughout the challenges of this journey. Your kindness, empathy, and wisdom have been a guiding light, helping me navigate the complexities of parenthood. Your encouragement and love have been my rock, and I am endlessly grateful for your presence in my life.

Together, you have enriched my world, teaching me the profound lessons of resilience, compassion, and unconditional love. This book stands as a testament to the invaluable gifts you have bestowed upon me.

Forever grateful,
MOM.

SECTION A

INTRODUCTION: UNDERSTANDING ADHD — A PARENT'S JOURNEY

In the quiet moments of dusk, as the world hushed into slumber, my world often echoed with the vibrant energy of my son. His laughter echoed through the halls, his curiosity an unstoppable force, his boundless spirit a sight to behold. Yet, amidst this whirlwind of energy, I found myself navigating uncharted waters—the world of ADHD.

My name is Sakina Kagalwala, and this book is a reflection of my journey alongside my son, who has taught me more about life and resilience than any classroom ever could. It's a story woven with the threads of personal experiences, trials, and triumphs, one that resonates with countless parents striving to understand and support their children with ADHD.

Before I delved into the world of ADHD, it was a nebulous concept, a mere acronym in a sea of medical terms. Little did I realize the depth of its impact, and the challenges it posed not just to my son but to our entire family. ADHD, or Attention-Deficit/Hyperactivity Disorder, is a multifaceted condition that transcends mere inattentiveness or impulsivity. It's a complex interplay of cognitive processes and behavioural patterns that require a nuanced understanding.

In the first chapters of this book, I invite you to walk in my shoes—to witness the highs and lows, the moments of frustration, and the flashes of sheer brilliance that define our lives. But beyond our personal narrative lies a deeper exploration—a journey into the heart of ADHD itself. What follows is an exploration of what ADHD truly is— an amalgamation of neurological intricacies, societal perceptions, and the lived experiences of those affected by it. We'll dissect its nuances, unravel the misconceptions, and understand the challenges faced not just by children with ADHD but by their parents as well.

Navigating the labyrinth of ADHD can be an overwhelming endeavour. Parents, like myself, grapple with a multitude of questions, uncertainties, and daily struggles. From the baffling maze of diagnoses to the stigma and misconceptions clouding this condition, we've encountered hurdles that seemed insurmountable.

However, this book isn't just about challenges; it's about empowerment and resilience. It's a repository of insights gleaned from research, expert opinions, and, most importantly, the collective wisdom of parents who have walked similar paths. It's a testament to the fact that while ADHD may pose hurdles, it also gifts us with unique perspectives and unparalleled strengths.

The latter sections of this book delve into strategies and techniques—tools honed through trial and error, and wisdom forged through perseverance. Managing ADHD behaviour isn't a one-size-fits-all approach; it's an intricate tapestry woven with patience, understanding, and a relentless pursuit of what works best for each unique child.

As we embark on this journey together, I invite you to open your mind and heart. Whether you're a parent, a caregiver, an educator, or someone seeking to understand the world of ADHD, let these pages serve as a beacon of hope and enlightenment.

Join me as we navigate the labyrinth of ADHD, unravel its complexities, and emerge armed with knowledge, empathy, and a renewed sense of purpose—a purpose to support, nurture, and celebrate the extraordinary individuals who defy the odds every day.

Welcome to the world of ADHD—a world of challenges, triumphs, and boundless possibilities.

SECTION B

"UNVEILING THE JOURNEY: RAISING A SON WITH ADHD - TRIALS, TRIUMPHS, AND UNWAVERING LOVE"

Life's journey often unfolds in unexpected ways, challenging us with twists and turns we never envisioned. My path took a distinctive route the moment my son entered the world—a vibrant, curious soul wired with boundless energy and an uncontainable spirit. Little did I know that his diagnosis of Attention Deficit Hyperactivity Disorder (ADHD) would not only redefine my understanding of parenthood but also lead me through a labyrinth of trials and triumphs, reshaping my perceptions, resilience, and capacity for empathy.

Raising a child with ADHD became a transformative Chapter in my life, one that was brimming with joy, and love, but also an array of hurdles that seemed insurmountable at times. As I reflect on this journey, I'm compelled to share the intricacies, the struggles, and the profound lessons that have unfolded along the way. It's a story of perseverance, acceptance, and the unwavering bond between a parent and a child navigating the turbulent waters of ADHD. Join me as I unveil the poignant narrative of my journey raising a son with ADHD—a journey marked by challenges that ultimately led to growth, understanding, and unyielding love.

Chapter 1

"From Chaos to Joy: Navigating Parenthood with a Sleepless Newborn"

At the break of dawn on a crisp August morning, a surge of agony gripped my abdomen. It was the 22nd, my ninth month - a crucial time. By 3 pm, the pain crescendoed into an unbearable symphony of contractions. It wasn't just any pain; it was the telltale sign of impending delivery.

Amidst this whirlwind, a flood of thoughts inundated my mind. My 5-year-old daughter waited expectantly at home, while my father-in-law, battling stage 4 cancer, awaited his soup—a routine I had meticulously set in motion. Racing against time, torn between responsibilities, I made a decision.

Returning home was non-negotiable. My heart ached to leave them, but I knew I had to ensure their comfort before my own. The scene at home was one of controlled chaos, every detail meticulously tended to. Yet, my pain escalated beyond control, eclipsing everything else.

Amidst screams of agony, my husband's trembling presence, and the chorus of voices urging me to leave for the hospital, I hesitated. But there was no denying the urgency. The rush to the hospital was a blur, each moment agonizingly etched with pain.

Admitted swiftly, the doctor's astonishment was palpable—a six-inch opening already. In just an hour, amidst the commotion and disbelief, my little bundle of joy entered the world, a beacon of pure bliss. All worries and all pains dissolved when I beheld him— healthy, radiant, and content.

Yet, amidst the joy, a tiny wrinkle in our happiness emerged—he refused to sleep.

And so, the story of my son began, a journey marked by unexpected twists and the unrelenting challenge of sleeplessness. Amidst the chaos and uncertainties, his arrival heralded a new chapter—a tale woven with love, resilience, and the unspoken promise of boundless joy.

Chapter 2

"Unstoppable Whirlwinds: Navigating Parenthood with a Child Full of Boundless Energy and ADHD"

Imagine a world where sleep was a luxury, where days blurred into nights with a restless, unstoppable force at the centre - my son, an enigmatic bundle of energy. His early years unfolded like a puzzle, each piece a sign pointing towards something I couldn't quite grasp - signs of ADHD hidden in plain sight.

From colic aids to vaporubs and unconventional remedies, I chased elusive sleep for my son, unaware that his tireless spirit was an early indicator of the journey we were about to embark on. By the age of three, he'd transformed our routine into a whirlwind of laughter, chaos, and endless adventure, leaving me both exhausted and exhilarated.

In this whirlwind, I found myself at a crossroads, torn between yearning for a moment's rest and craving a sense of normalcy beyond our wild days. The choices I faced were as complex as they were universal - a dance between self-care and the unyielding love and dedication demanded by a child with boundless energy.

Chapter 3

"Embracing Motherhood: Shattering the Supermom Myth, Finding Support, and Rediscovering Self Care"

Enrolling my son in a play school was a hopeful leap, a tiny step towards a change that I desperately yearned for. Miraculously, it worked. Those precious moments after school when he slept for a mere 20-30 minutes became a lifeline for me. In that fleeting time, I became a whirlwind, a mom with the speed and agility of the Flash, racing against the clock to tackle chores and responsibilities.

But amidst this dizzying pace, a haunting question lingered: why do we, as mothers, habitually don the cape of a superhero? Why does the weight of responsibilities often fall solely on our shoulders, leaving us hesitant to ask for support or share the load?

Society's expectations, like a silent force, press down on us, compelling us to carry on without a pause. But it's time for a shift. It's time for understanding, for society to extend a helping hand to new mothers rather than simply prescribing remedies. Instead of solely judging a mother's actions, why not empathize with her experiences as a woman navigating the labyrinth of motherhood?

And it's not just society—women too need to embrace a new narrative. Motherhood is undoubtedly a transformative journey, but it doesn't mandate the sacrifice of our individual stories. We are still individuals deserving of "me time" and moments of respite. Why should every waking second revolve solely around motherhood? It's crucial to not lose ourselves completely in this new chapter.

Let's shatter the myth of the supermom and instead celebrate the strength in asking for help, in sharing responsibilities, and in prioritizing self-care. It's time to be kinder to ourselves, to acknowledge that being a mother is just one facet of our identity, not the sum of it all.

Chapter 4

"Navigating Parenthood: Unveiling the Challenges of Learning Disabilities, Communication, and ADHD in Children"

Every school day felt like a marathon, a two-hour vigil outside the school gates, a silent reassurance to my son that I was there, by his side, in this new and daunting space. While his classmates effortlessly navigated conversations, my son struggled to find his voice. It was the first glimpse into a larger challenge—his struggle with a learning difficulty.

Amid my worries, everyone had advice—karela juice, a parrot's bite, tongue injections—each idea more confusing than the last. But I stood firm, believing in my child, ignoring the chaotic remedies.

This chaos is something that many mothers often face—the world buzzing with opinions that only serve to heighten anxiety, casting shadows on the already stressed mind of a mother. In these moments, it's the challenge to remain composed, to believe, and to act with unwavering resolve.

My approach was simple yet profound—I immersed my son in books of his choosing, reading to him daily. Cartoons and videos became a treasure trove of vocabulary, aiding his journey to find his voice. Small victories followed, with encouragement for him to articulate simple words like "yes" and "no." Slowly, but steadily, my son began to communicate, opening doors to a world of words.

But as one hurdle was overcome, another emerged. His newfound ability to express himself abundantly, to talk incessantly, raised another flag—this time, a sign of ADHD. It left me grappling with a perplexing paradox. Was speaking too little a problem before, and now, speaking too much is an issue? The constant assessment of milestones and the need to fit every aspect of our children into predefined parameters left me questioning.

Why can't we simply let our children be? Why must every milestone be scrutinized? These unanswered questions linger, echoing the struggle of countless mothers navigating the delicate balance between society's expectations and the untamed spirit of their children.

Chapter 5

"Navigating Parenthood Amidst COVID-19: Challenges, Uncertainties, and the Unyielding Quest for Child Well-being"

Amidst the joys of motherhood and the anticipation of a new Chapter balancing work and parenting, the unforeseen arrival of the deadly spectre, of COVID, altered the course of our lives abruptly. The world transformed, and we, unprepared, found ourselves navigating uncharted waters. What lay ahead was an unforeseen struggle that cast a shadow over our children's lives.

As we endeavoured to protect our families in a world suddenly defined by fear and uncertainty, the toll on our children's emotional, physiological, and intellectual well-being was staggering. The safe haven we once sought to create for them shattered as they grappled with the transition to a virtual existence—screens replacing classrooms, online games becoming companions, and routines dissolving into chaos.

Their once-boundless world shrank to the confines of gadgets, devoid of schedules, physical activity, or the enriching fabric of social interaction. We unwittingly confined them to a small, sheltered reality. And the price they paid was immense. After two arduous years, children emerged bearing a heavy burden—ADHD, dyslexia, learning disabilities, anxiety, anger issues, a sense of insecurity, and weakened immune systems, among a litany of other challenges.

In my role as a counsellor, I witnessed the anguish and fear in the hearts of countless mothers, offering solace while grappling with the same uncertainties within myself. The looming concern that gnawed at me—my son, unprepared for the world that awaited him. Unable to read or write, and struggling to focus, he found himself a step behind his peers. How would he navigate this new reality? Protecting his self-esteem became my unwavering priority, but in a world so unpredictable, was it an attainable goal for every mother?

Amidst these uncertainties, questions echoed relentlessly. Should we shield our children from these adversities or let them confront the world's harsh realities? Are we being too stringent in our protective embrace? The truth remains elusive, leaving us stranded in a limbo of uncertainty.

Despite the lack of clear answers, life propels us forward. We must accept the present and navigate the uncertain path ahead, understanding and acknowledging the challenges that lie in wait, as we endeavour to find solace and purpose amidst the unknown.

Chapter 6

"Motherhood's Balancing Act: Navigating ADHD, LD, and the Quest for Solutions Amidst Challenges"

While watching my son navigate through what seemed like an intricate maze of challenges, I found myself lost in contemplation. Was it ADHD or LD, or perhaps something entirely different? Until then, I had been his anchor, working tirelessly with him, relying on my instincts and knowledge. The fear of an assessment loomed over me like a dark cloud; I trembled at the thought of taking that decisive step toward a diagnosis and potential treatment. Nights were often soaked in silent tears, yet by morning, I wore a facade of strength.

Eventually, summoning every ounce of courage, I took the daunting leap, seeking counsel from an occupational therapist and initiating the evaluation. The result mirrored my deepest apprehensions—my son was diagnosed with ADHD and LD. Despite the foreboding, we commenced occupational therapy without delay. I approached his school, confiding in his class teacher about his condition. Her reassurances, though comforting, didn't quell my worries entirely. For a whole year, my world revolved solely around my son. I immersed myself in relentless research, fervently seeking understanding and ways to aid his progress.

This, I realized, is what mothers do—we construct castles for our children, undeterred by the modest dwellings we inhabit ourselves. My days were a whirlwind, commencing with teaching him the basics, navigating from one extracurricular class to another—football, karate, skating, swimming—anything to channel his boundless energy. I was drained, physically and emotionally, yet propelled by an unyielding determination to help him. But in my fervour, I lost sight of his desires. My vision was clouded by a relentless storm of concerns and anxieties.

I strived to prepare him for the world, not to compete but to equip him for every challenge it might offer. Yet, amidst my noble intentions, I demanded too much of both myself and my son. It's a tale often shared by mothers—we become so fixated on the problems that the solutions slip from our view, veiled by our unwavering determination to make things right.

Chapter 7

"Rediscovering Joy: a Mother's Journey of Sacrifice, Realization, and Prioritizing Happiness in Parenthood"

Without realizing it, my dedication had worn me out. Exhaustion crept in, leaving me irritable and frustrated. I was pushing myself too hard, but I didn't see it. It took my husband's keen eye to notice.

"Take a break," he said, worried. "You're doing too much. You're making things harder unintentionally." At first, I was hurt. How could he doubt all the years I'd spent working hard and sacrificing? But in his words was a truth I couldn't see—the truth we miss when we focus only on the goal and forget the journey.

As I struggled, my son's troubles broke my heart. He'd come home in tears, teased and struggling to keep up. His confidence was shaken by others' laughter. It was a pain only a mom could understand, something the world often misses.

In this chaos, I realized something big: my son wasn't happy. He was drowning in everyone's expectations, and I was his only support. No coaching or therapy could fix his spirit. That's when I decided to stop everything. I wanted his happiness more than anything.

Football, skating, karate, therapy—everything came to a standstill. The following day, as he returned home disheartened, expecting another class, I uttered the words he least expected: "No class today, go play freely." His eyes lit up, a spark of joy that ignited his spirit. His radiant smile, a treasure I had longed for, changed the trajectory of our lives.

In that fleeting moment, everything shifted. I realized that happiness wasn't found in schedules or achievements but in the pure freedom to play, to be carefree, and to relish the sheer joy of childhood. And in that moment, I found solace, witnessing my child's happiness becomes the compass guiding our new journey.

Chapter 8

"Embracing Passion: A Mother's Journey from Overwhelm to Clarity, Cultivating Joy in Parenthood"

Amidst all the confusion, one thing was crystal clear—I wanted to see my son's bright smile. So, I made a decision to keep things simple. I let go of the pressure and just let him be.

In that moment of respite, I finally comprehended the essence of my husband's advice. Just like an overloaded computer that freezes, sometimes, you need to switch it off and restart—disconnecting momentarily to reset. That's precisely what I was doing—creating a sanctuary, shielding ourselves from life's complexities to bask in the serenity of normalcy. His happiness became my solace; it nurtured my own.

Taking a leap forward, I resumed my role as a counsellor in a hospital. Helping others brought me unparalleled joy. Empowered by my own experiences, I connected with mothers on a profound level, understanding their struggles and offering guidance with newfound empathy. This transformative phase brought a surge in my clientele, expanding my work, and satiating my soul with contentment and happiness.

Amidst this renewed sense of purpose, clarity emerged. I rediscovered my passion and found myself better equipped to understand my son's aspirations. A seemingly ordinary evening unfolded, the soft glow of my laptop casting a comforting aura. There, in the living room, my son revealed the simple pleasure of running. "Why run?" I questioned, concerned he might tire himself out. His response was a revelation—running was his joy, his strength.

At that moment, clarity struck like lightning. His love for running was unmistakable, a passion ingrained in him since infancy. Athletics seemed a natural path. I broached the subject delicately, offering him the freedom to explore without pressure. His assurance, his promise to find joy, filled my heart with warmth.

Enrolling him in athletics was a pivotal decision—one grounded in his interests, not societal expectations. I emphasized his journey, assuring him it wasn't about comparisons but his personal growth. His enthusiasm flourished, his focus sharpened, and his speed surged—not because he had to, but because he embraced what he loved.

Chapter 9

"Discovering Joy in Growth: a Mother's Transformational Journey with Her Child"

As my son got into sports, I found a sweet spot balancing his athletics and helping him with reading and writing. It wasn't about fitting him into a box; it was about making him content with his skills. Sometimes, a change in how we see things can work wonders.

His progress mirrored my shift. His grades went from a so-so C to a solid B, making him super happy. His teacher's praise lit up his face, giving him a boost. Each win made him more sure of himself like a kid finding his way.

Among these wins, swimming became a new thing—an oasis where healing flowed as smoothly as the water. Swimming became therapy, a place for both emotional and physical healing. Our time in the water was more than strokes; it was about healing and having fun together. That's when I realized I had the wrong focus before. It wasn't about him being a great swimmer; it was about finding peace and healing, and he showed that in every moment.

I had an aha moment—a realization that came from what we went through together. I made mistakes before, but it's never too late to change. Life gives us chances to fix things and learn from what we've been through. None of us starts as experts; we all learn and grow as we go along this journey called life.

Chapter 10

"Empowering Motherhood: Navigating Challenges, Embracing Vulnerability, and Finding Joy in the Journey"

Dear fellow travellers on this journey of motherhood,

I share my story not to stand apart but to stand together with each of you. Our paths, though unique, often intersect in moments of anxiety, despair, and fatigue. There's a silent camaraderie among us—mothers who've weathered storms of anxiety, depression, and a myriad of emotions. We stumble, make mistakes, and at times, feel utterly vulnerable. There are days when the weight of it all makes us want to flee, to escape the overwhelming reality we're navigating.

But please, do not carry the weight of guilt or self-blame. You are not alone in this; it's not a failing on your part. You are doing your utmost, pouring every ounce of knowledge and love into nurturing your child. There's immense strength in that.

In the upcoming chapters of this book, I aim to delve deeper into the intricacies of managing our emotions—the ebbs and flows that accompany this journey. I'll share insights on helping your child realize their full potential and finding that delicate balance between work, home, and the beautiful chaos of raising kids. But more importantly, I'll explore the art of finding happiness in every situation life throws our way.

We are a tapestry of experiences, woven together by our struggles and triumphs. Together, let's navigate this journey, offering support, understanding, and the unwavering belief that amidst the challenges, there's an abundance of strength and love within us.

SECTION C

"EXPLORING THE DIFFERENT TYPES OF ADHD AND THEIR CHARACTERISTICS"

Most children experience times when their behaviour becomes uncontrollable. They may refuse to wait their turn, shout and scream, cry, roll on the floor, crash into objects, break things, become lost in daydreams, or become inattentive. However, some children experience these behaviours more frequently and severely than others. Children with ADHD face such behavioural issues so often and severely that it interferes with their ability to live a normal life.

It is imperative to gain an understanding of the fundamental characteristics of ADHD. The three primary areas of focus are inattention, hyperactivity, and impulsivity, with all other behavioural patterns being subordinate to these three traits. It is critical to recognize that these characteristics can significantly impact an individual's daily life and can lead to difficulties in academics. Therefore, it is essential to develop a thorough comprehension of ADHD to provide appropriate support and management strategies for those affected by this neurodevelopmental disorder.

It's important to acknowledge that children may not always have complete control over their behaviour. Sometimes, they act without thinking of the consequences. It can be challenging to deal with, but it's crucial to understand that they may not be able to help it. Patience is key in these situations, even though it can be exhausting both mentally and emotionally. Remember that your child learns from you, so showing empathy and understanding can go a long way.

Types of ADHD

As we know ADHD is characterized by inattentiveness and hyperactivity, On, this basis ADHD is divided into 3 main types

1. Kids who are inattentive but not hyperactive, also called ADD [attention deficit disorder]
2. Kids who are hyperactive but not inattentive
3. Kids who are inattentive and hyperactive both

In ADD, in the inattentive type, the child faces more problems with attention and fewer problems related to hyperactivity. For example, getting distracted easily, getting bored, having trouble focusing, trouble following instructions, being unable to listen and interpret or recollect, daydreaming, and losing things very often.

Parents often fail to recognize certain symptoms in their children, unless the school raises concerns. It's only when a child is unable to keep up with their peers and feels overwhelmed that they might either give up or have an emotional outburst. Unfortunately, until then, these children are often labelled as lazy or unintelligent, which can lead them to accept this negative self-image and hinder their motivation to improve.

In the second type of situation, children may be impulsive and hyperactive. They have difficulty sitting still, fidget with objects, are fearless, prone to accidents, often break things unintentionally, talk a lot, ask too many questions, never seem to tire, are impatient, and need frequent changes of activity.

Children who exhibit impulsive behaviour are often viewed as troublemakers with low expectations set for them. They are frequently criticized and prevented from doing things, which only serves to increase their curiosity and hyperactivity.

Children with ADHD often exhibit problems with inattentiveness and hyperactivity. The combined type, which is a combination of type 1 and type 2, can cause difficulties in various settings such as home, school, and social activities. The symptoms can vary from child to child, and some may display overlapping characteristics. This type of ADHD can affect day-to-day life activities and requires proper management.

Co Existing Conditions

There are some common co-existing conditions with ADHD.

1. **Learning Difficulty [LD]**: It's important to understand that LD, or learning disability, is a condition that can make it challenging for a child to read, learn, or write. It's worth noting that not all children with ADHD will experience Learning disability. Sometimes, children may simply have learning difficulties. It's essential to differentiate between learning disability and learning difficulty. Disability refers to intellectual disability, which may arise from various factors such as genetic factors, events in the prenatal or post-natal period, or any other neurological impairment. On the other hand, learning difficulty refers to one's inability to acquire and use language in verbal, nonverbal, and written form. The good news is that learning difficulties can be reversed. If your child faces problems with reading or writing, or both, such as difficulty holding a pencil properly, forming letters, illegible handwriting, confusion with upper case and lower case letters, trouble pronouncing words, or difficulty in understanding the sound of words, it's crucial to address these issues as soon as possible. Learning disabilities

(LD) may manifest in various ways, such as an inability to read or write. It is also possible for a child to experience difficulties with math, despite exhibiting proficiency in reading and writing. The specific type of LD that a child may have can vary, and each requires a unique approach to diagnosis and treatment.

2. **Mood Disorders**: Children with ADHD often struggle to manage their emotions, which can lead to mood disorders such as depression and suicidal tendencies during their teenage years if not properly assisted. They may also feel lonely and isolated due to difficulty with social interactions and may face bullying from peers. The constant negative feedback from school can break their confidence, and not all teachers have the patience and empathy needed to support them. Inattentiveness can also lead to difficulties following rules in games and making friends. These children are often sensitive and require a lot of love and understanding.

3. **ODD:** Oppositional Defiant Disorder or ODD is a condition that is characterized by children losing their temper easily, intentionally annoying others, and being hostile. This condition is more common in children who also have

hyperactivity and impulsivity. Due to their hyperactivity, children with ODD may have difficulty controlling their anger. When feeling rejected or unaccepted, they may break rules or even engage in self-harm or harm towards others. Managing such behaviour requires a lot of care and mindfulness. It is essential to be aware of the words and actions we use while dealing with children with ODD.

4. **Anxiety Disorder**: Anxiety is a common issue among children with ADHD, where they experience extreme feelings of fear, worry, and a constant sense of being judged. These intense emotions often lead to physical symptoms such as nausea, sweating, stomach aches, and headaches. Children with ADHD often fear being bullied, misunderstood, judged, and unaccepted, leading to low self-esteem. It is important to support and encourage these children, boost their confidence, and help them manage their anxiety.

Overall, it's crucial to provide children with the support they need to feel safe and accepted. By working with professionals who specialize in these areas, children can learn valuable skills and strategies to help them thrive both in and out of the classroom. With, proper and timely intervention we can help the child deal with his limitations and help him focus on his strengths.

SECTION D

"UNDERSTANDING THE FACTORS THAT CONTRIBUTE TO ADHD: A COMPREHENSIVE GUIDE"

Attention-deficit/hyperactivity disorder (ADHD) is a complex neurodevelopmental disorder that can be influenced by a variety of factors. These factors can interact in different ways, making it difficult to pinpoint a single cause for ADHD. Here are some of the key factors that are believed to contribute to the development and manifestation of ADHD:

Chapter 1

Genetic Factors

Attention Deficit Hyperactivity Disorder (ADHD) has been found to have a substantial genetic component. Studies indicate that ADHD frequently runs in families, suggesting a strong hereditary influence. Research has identified specific genes that are associated with neurotransmitter regulation and brain development, which have been implicated in the development of ADHD.

Chapter 2

Brain Structure and Function

Differences in brain structure and function can contribute to ADHD. Studies have shown that individuals with ADHD may have differences in the size and activity of certain brain regions, particularly those involved in attention, impulse control, and executive functions.

Many of the characteristics of ADHD are related to executive functioning. This refers to a set of mental skills that include working memory, emotional control, and complex problem-solving. Essentially, executive functions are the skills we all use to manage day-to-day tasks, such as time management, staying organized, and planning. While several different parts of the brain contribute to executive functioning, the prefrontal cortex is especially important in regulating these skills.

Research has shown that in children with ADHD, the prefrontal cortex matures more slowly than in typically developing kids. It is also slightly smaller in size. Similarly, the cerebellum, hippocampus, and amygdala are also thought to be smaller in volume in kids with ADHD.

Like every part of the brain, the cerebellum is involved in many different functions, but its role in the regulation of movement may be especially relevant to ADHD symptoms. A smaller cerebellum could contribute to difficulty with what's called "motor response inhibition," which refers to the ability to suppress actions that interfere with a current task, such as staying seated during a class lesson. Smaller hippocampus and amygdala sizes can cause impairment in the regulation of memory, emotion, and behaviour, which is a common symptom of kids with ADHD.

While these regions of the brain may remain smaller in people with ADHD, studies have shown that they do continue to grow and mature as children get older. By adulthood, the difference in size when compared to individuals without the disorder has appeared to be less significant.

Chapter 3

Neurotransmitter Imbalance

Dysregulation of certain neurotransmitters, such as dopamine and norepinephrine, is thought to be involved in ADHD. These neurotransmitters play a key role in regulating attention, impulse control, and motivation.

Serving as our control centre, the brain needs to both send and receive electrical signals or "messages" throughout the body. The brain can do this via nerve cells (neurons). However, there are gaps between neurons. Neurotransmitters are the chemical messengers that fill the gap and allow for messages to be passed along.

One very important neurotransmitter is dopamine, which has several functions. There are pathways in the brain that allow the transport of dopamine from one region to another to relay important information. In children with ADHD, these pathways are thought to be disrupted, which can lead to impairment of cognitive and motivational functioning. Scientists believe that these disruptions could be due to an unusual number of dopamine transporters in the brains of people with ADHD. A dopamine transporter is a protein that is responsible for removing dopamine from the gap between neurons and terminating dopamine transmission. An increased number of these transporters can lead to unusually low amounts of dopamine in the brain.

Chapter 4

Prenatal and Perinatal Factors

Prenatal and perinatal factors are events and conditions that occur during pregnancy and around the time of birth, which can potentially influence the risk of ADHD (Attention-Deficit/ Hyperactivity Disorder) in children. While not all children exposed to these factors will develop ADHD, they are considered risk factors. Some of the prenatal and perinatal factors associated with an increased risk of ADHD in children include:

- **Maternal Smoking:** Smoking during pregnancy is a significant risk factor for ADHD. Nicotine and other toxins in tobacco smoke can affect fetal brain development and increase the likelihood of ADHD symptoms.

- **Alcohol and Substance Use:** Maternal consumption of alcohol or illicit drugs during pregnancy can lead to developmental problems, including an increased risk of ADHD in the child.

- **Premature Birth:** Preterm birth (birth before 37 weeks of gestation) and low birth weight are associated with an elevated risk of ADHD. These factors may disrupt normal brain development.

- **Complications During Pregnancy:** Various complications during pregnancy, such as gestational diabetes, preeclampsia, and maternal infections, have been linked to a higher risk of ADHD in the child.

- **Exposure to Environmental Toxins:** Prenatal exposure to environmental toxins like lead and polychlorinated biphenyls (PCBs) has been associated with an increased risk of ADHD. Lead exposure, in particular, can impair cognitive and behavioural functions.

- **Maternal Stress and Depression:** High levels of maternal stress, anxiety, and depression during pregnancy have been linked to an increased risk of ADHD in offspring. Chronic stress during pregnancy can affect fetal development, including the brain.

- **Malnutrition and Poor Diet:** Inadequate prenatal nutrition and exposure to an unhealthy diet during pregnancy may contribute to ADHD risk. Some studies suggest that maternal malnutrition or diets lacking essential nutrients may affect fetal brain development.

- **Infections During Pregnancy:** Certain maternal infections, such as rubella or cytomegalovirus, can pose a risk to the developing fetal brain and have been associated with ADHD in some cases.

- **Complications During Birth:** Birth complications, such as fetal distress or oxygen deprivation during delivery, may increase the risk of ADHD, although the relationship is not always straightforward.

It's important to note that these factors, while associated with an increased risk of ADHD, do not guarantee that a child will develop the disorder. ADHD is a complex condition influenced by multiple genetic and environmental factors, and its precise causes are not fully understood.

Additionally, while these prenatal and perinatal factors may increase the risk of ADHD, early intervention and appropriate management can help mitigate the impact of ADHD symptoms in children. Parents and healthcare providers should work together to provide support and treatment for children with ADHD, regardless of the presence of these risk factors.

Chapter 5

External Factors

When it comes to attention deficit hyperactivity disorder (ADHD), you may wonder whether nature or nurture plays the largest role in causing it.

Environmental factors don't directly cause ADHD. At least, not on their own.

Genetics plays a big role. But your environment can also contain factors that lead to ADHD.

These environmental factors can include:

- **Early life experiences:** Early childhood experiences, such as trauma, neglect, or significant adversity, can contribute to the development of ADHD symptoms. Chronic stress and adverse childhood experiences may affect brain development and function.

- **Nutritional diet:** While diet alone is not a direct cause of ADHD, some studies suggest that certain dietary factors may influence ADHD symptoms. For example, a diet high in sugar and artificial food additives, and packaged food that contains a high amount of artificial colours, flavours, and preservatives may exacerbate symptoms in some individuals.

- **Other mental health conditions:** Other mental health conditions such as anxiety, depression, and learning disabilities, often co-occur with ADHD. These conditions can complicate diagnosis and treatment.
- **Social factors:** The demands of modern society, such as academic and workplace expectations, can place additional stress on individuals with ADHD. Supportive environments and accommodations can help individuals with ADHD succeed.

It's important to note that ADHD is a heterogeneous condition, and the factors contributing to it can vary from person to person. Additionally, there is ongoing research in this field, and our understanding of the factors influencing ADHD continues to evolve. Diagnosis and management of ADHD typically involve a comprehensive assessment by healthcare professionals and may include a combination of behavioural therapies, medication, and educational interventions tailored to the individual's specific needs.

SECTION E

UNDERSTANDING ADHD

Chapter 1

Diagnosis and Assessment

As a trusted assistant, I often receive a common concern from parents regarding their child's potential ADHD diagnosis. Parents often ask me how they can determine if their child has ADHD, as well as what the next steps should be and where they can go for help. Unfortunately, there is still limited knowledge about the diagnosis of ADHD and LD in children, which can lead to parents unknowingly mistaking their child's struggles for laziness or a lack of interest. These misconceptions can have a damaging impact on the child's self-esteem and hinder their academic and social growth.

It is essential to identify the symptoms of ADHD early on, so children can receive the necessary treatment and support. To accomplish this, workshops should be held in schools to educate parents about ADHD and LD, and how to identify potential symptoms in their children. By identifying areas where the child is facing difficulties, analysing their behaviour patterns, and determining if they have ADHD, parents can guide their child to receive appropriate support and treatment.

To identify ADHD in children, parents should observe their child's behaviour and see if they display at least 6 or more symptoms consistently for several months. It is crucial to note that children may face temporary attention problems due to external factors like stress or anxiety, but if the symptoms persist, it's best to seek professional help.

In conclusion, parents must pay attention to the signs and symptoms of ADHD in their children, and take the necessary steps to provide proper support and treatment. By working together with schools and professionals, parents can help their children overcome these challenges and achieve their full potential.

Signs and Symptoms of ADHD:

1. The child seems to have difficulty retaining information, as they frequently forget where they have placed their belongings or what they have learned in school. They may also struggle to remember conversations or instructions given to them before sleeping.
2. The child appears to have a restlessness that prevents them from sitting still for extended

periods. They may feel compelled to move, run, or jump frequently.

3. The child has a fidgety nature and feels the need to be occupied at all times. They struggle to sit idle and may require constant stimulation.

4. The child has difficulty focusing on tasks for extended periods and may become easily distracted by external stimuli, such as noises or conversations.

5. The child speaks impulsively and asks many questions without considering the context or appropriateness of their inquiries.

6. The child may struggle to follow multiple instructions given to them at home or in school, such as changing clothes, washing their hands, or completing specific tasks.

7. This child seems to avoid or dislike activities that require significant effort or attention, such as puzzles, reading, or writing.

8. The child appears impatient and may struggle to wait for answers or their turn in a queue.

9. The child seems to become bored easily and may require constant stimulation.

10. The individual may make careless mistakes, such as falling or injuring themselves due to their distracted behaviour.

11. This child may struggle to complete tasks on time due to their inability to focus and become easily distracted.

12. The child appears to have a disturbed sleep pattern, as they may struggle to fall asleep or remain asleep for a full night's rest.

13. The child may struggle with fine motor skills, such as tying shoelaces or buttoning clothing.

14. The child may have difficulty holding a pencil or writing due to poor finger grip or too much or too little pressure.

15. The child may exhibit extreme emotional behaviour, such as being overly aggressive or sensitive and easily becoming cranky.

16. The child may struggle with organizational skills, such as maintaining a tidy living space or keeping track of their belongings.

17. The child may speak loudly and continuously without regard for others around them.

18. The child may become easily agitated, and frustrated, and experience anger issues.

19. The child may exhibit behaviours such as clapping or tapping their feet frequently.

20. The child may be intolerant of specific sounds or sights, becoming easily overwhelmed or distressed.

21. Occasionally, this child may become hyper-focused on a specific task or activity to the point of losing track of everything else around them.
22. The child may have a negative self-image due to poor academic performance, leading to a poor perception of themselves.
23. This child may lack motivation due to low confidence and self-doubt.

If you happen to observe certain telltale signs in your child, there is a significant possibility that they may need to be assessed for Attention Deficit Hyperactivity Disorder (ADHD). Upon observing any such symptoms, it is essential to have your child formally evaluated by a professional practitioner. Consulting with a special educator who is trained to conduct an assessment to determine whether your child has ADHD is recommended. To navigate this process successfully, it is important to understand the roles played by different medical practitioners in this field.

Chapter 2

Roles Played By Different Medical Practitioners

Psychiatrist/ Developmental Paediatrician:

In the event of a child being diagnosed with ADHD, a paediatrician or psychiatrist may prescribe medication as part of a comprehensive treatment plan that accounts for the child's individual needs. Medication can be effective in managing symptoms such as hyperactivity and impulsivity, but it is important to note that the effects of medication can vary from child to child and that there may be some side effects.

It is crucial to work closely with a healthcare professional to determine the appropriate medication for your child. A paediatrician or psychiatrist will consider factors such as the child's age, weight, and medical history, as well as any other co-occurring conditions such as anxiety, mood disorders, learning disabilities, seizures, or sleep problems. They may also conduct regular check-ins to monitor the child's response to the medication and adjust the dosage or medication type as needed.

It is worth noting that medication is not a permanent solution for ADHD, but rather a tool to help manage symptoms and facilitate the learning and practice of new skills. A child may respond positively to one medication but not to another, which is why working closely with a healthcare professional is crucial in finding the right medication for your child. It is also important to ensure that the child is receiving appropriate behavioural therapy and support from family, teachers, and other healthcare professionals to address any non-medical aspects of ADHD.

Psychologist/ Counsellor:

As parents, we all want the best for our children, but sometimes we can encounter obstacles that are beyond our control. ADHD is a common neurodevelopmental disorder that affects many children. Fortunately, there are counsellors who provide specialized psychotherapy and behavioural therapy sessions to help children with ADHD develop coping skills, emotional regulation, and improved impulse control.

Counsellors work closely with ADHD children to identify specific areas of difficulty, such as time management, organization, and social skills, which are often impaired in individuals with ADHD. With care and patience, counsellors help children to learn and develop these skills, which can be crucial for their success both in school and in life.

In addition to skill-building, counsellors also help children to regulate their emotions. Children with ADHD are often prone to anger outbursts, mood swings, and depression. Counsellors provide a safe and supportive environment for children to express their feelings and work through their emotions.

But counsellors don't just work with children - they also work with parents. Parent training programs are common interventions that offer emotional support to both the child and their family, helping them navigate the challenges and stigma associated with ADHD. Counsellors equip parents with strategies to manage their child's ADHD-related behaviours at home and in school, providing guidance and support every step of the way.

If your child is struggling with ADHD, know that you are not alone. With the help of counsellors, children with ADHD can learn to thrive and reach their full potential.

Occupational Therapist:

ADHD often face several challenges in their daily lives. Occupational therapists play a significant role in the holistic and multidisciplinary approach to addressing the needs of these children. They work towards helping children develop the skills and strategies necessary to navigate daily life effectively, manage their symptoms, and thrive in various environments.

To achieve this, occupational therapists conduct comprehensive assessments to understand the specific challenges and strengths of each child with ADHD. They evaluate sensory processing, motor skills, executive functioning, and self-regulation abilities, which are often affected in children with ADHD. Based on these assessments, occupational therapists create individualized treatment plans tailored to the unique needs of each child.

Occupational therapists work on improving a child's motor skills, which is a crucial aspect of their treatment plan. They focus on enhancing fine motor skills, such as handwriting, and gross motor skills, like balance and coordination, which can lead to better focus, organization, and participation in daily activities. With the help of occupational therapists, children with ADHD can learn to navigate their environment with greater ease and enjoy a more fulfilling life.

Remedial Therapist:

A Remedial Therapist is a professional who specializes in analysing a child's performance in various areas such as learning abilities, cognitive flexibility, behavioural responses, hyperactivity, and more. They employ scientifically designed therapy sessions and activities to help children overcome their difficulties and improve their skills in these areas. These therapy sessions and activities are customized to cater to each child's specific needs and are aimed at enhancing their cognitive, social, and emotional development. With their expertise and guidance, Remedial Therapists aid children in building their confidence and achieving academic success by addressing their individual challenges in a secure and supportive environment.

The management of ADHD requires the expertise of various professionals, including Psychiatrists, Occupational Therapists, Remedial Therapists, and Counsellors. Psychiatrists are responsible for conducting medical evaluations and managing medication, while counsellors specialize in behavioural therapy and skill-building. Occupational therapists utilize a multidisciplinary approach, and remedial therapists offer their unique expertise. Together, these professionals provide a comprehensive approach to ADHD management, addressing not only the core symptoms of the condition but also the emotional and social challenges that often accompany it. The collaborative effort of these professionals is essential in helping children with ADHD and their families lead fulfilling lives.

SECTION F

"UNTOLD STORIES: THE STRUGGLES AND TRIUMPHS OF PARENTS RAISING CHILDREN WITH ADHD"

Understandably, parents may feel overwhelmed when they discover that their child is having difficulties in areas where their peers seem to excel without any issues. It's an emotional rollercoaster for them. Parents of children with Attention-Deficit/Hyperactivity Disorder (ADHD) face significant challenges and the impact can be quite daunting.

Chapter 1

"Unveiling the Emotional Turmoil: The Rollercoaster of Parenting "

When confronted with the daily trials of managing their child's behaviours and academic difficulties, parents of children with ADHD often find themselves riding a tumultuous emotional rollercoaster. Overwhelm and frustration become unwelcome companions, and guilt can seep into the core of their being as they grapple with the inability to effortlessly "fix" their child's challenges. The questioning, the doubt, and the persistent thoughts of "why me?" and "why my child?" weave an intricate web of emotional distress.

Amongst the storms of emotions, mothers, in particular, can find themselves drowning in a sea of blame, their hearts heavy with the weight of perceived personal responsibility. The whispers of self-doubt can lead to a spiral into depression, as they question every decision, every action, and every missed opportunity to prevent their child from experiencing the difficulties associated with ADHD. The burdens of guilt become a constant companion, infiltrating their very being and clouding their ability to navigate the path ahead.

The societal pressure to meet certain benchmarks and comparisons with other children of the same age further exacerbate the emotional turmoil faced by parents. The incessant urge to measure their child's abilities against those of their peers can consume the minds of these parents, becoming an endless source of anxiety and distress. Thoughts like "Why can't my child be like the others?" or "Is there something I failed to do as a parent?" reverberate through the depths of their hearts, intensifying the emotional toll.

The unfortunate reality is that the emotional stress experienced by parents of children with ADHD is rarely discussed openly, contributing to their isolation in a world that can often seem unsympathetic. The weight of their emotions becomes a hidden burden, one that they carry silently, afraid to expose their vulnerability for fear of judgment or misunderstanding. Acknowledging the depth of these emotional struggles is crucial in fostering empathy and support for these parents, who are undoubtedly navigating uncharted waters.

Amidst the tempest of emotions, parents of children with ADHD need to seek solace and understanding. Encouraging open dialogue, whether it be through support groups, therapy, or simply connecting with other parents who share similar journeys, can provide a lifeline of understanding and solidarity. When these emotional burdens are shared, they become lighter, allowing for personal growth and resilience to flourish.

It is incumbent upon society to perceive and acknowledge the emotional turmoil that parents of children with ADHD endure. Awareness and education about the unique challenges these parents face can promote compassion and reduce judgment. By challenging stereotypes and offering avenues for support, we can create a safe space for parents to express their emotions and seek guidance, ultimately helping them develop the necessary resilience to navigate the intricate emotional landscape of raising a child with ADHD.

Parenting a child with ADHD is an undeniably demanding and emotionally charged endeavour. By embracing the reality of this emotional journey, by fostering empathy and understanding, we can help parents find strength and renewal. With the right support, they can traverse this rollercoaster of emotions, ultimately finding solace in the unwavering love and bond that exists between parent and child, regardless of the challenges they face.

"Navigating the Complexities of Parenting: a Struggle to Maintain Balance and Communication"

Raising a child with ADHD is an intricate journey that often puts a strain on the parent-child relationship. The delicate balance between enforcing discipline while simultaneously showing empathy and understanding can prove to be an ongoing challenge. These difficulties frequently result in heightened conflicts and strained communication between parent and child, deepening the sense of frustration experienced by parents.

Parents of children with ADHD often find it difficult to comprehend the complex and fluctuating symptoms associated with the disorder. This lack of understanding can hinder their ability to provide effective assistance, leading to a pervasive sense of helplessness and guilt. Watching their child struggle academically, behaviourally, or socially can trigger overwhelming feelings of frustration, amplifying the sense of anxiety, self-doubt, and even resentment within parents.

Like all parents, those raising children with ADHD have expectations for their child's development and success. However, when their child consistently falls short of these expectations due to the challenges posed by ADHD, it can lead to a cascade of negative emotions. Parents may question their own abilities as caregivers, feeling immense pressure to find solutions and "fix" their child's perceived shortcomings.

Moreover, the constant juggling act involved in parenting a child with ADHD can result in exhaustion and isolation. The never-ending effort to manage their child's symptoms, such as impulsivity, hyperactivity, and inattention, leaves little time or energy for self-care or personal pursuits. This perpetual state of being consumed by the responsibilities of raising a child with ADHD often leaves parents feeling physically and mentally drained, further amplifying the emotional burden they carry.

Recognizing that their child's behaviour and difficulties are not a reflection of their own worth as parents is also essential. Parents need to celebrate their victories, no matter how small, and acknowledge that progress is a journey filled with ups and downs. Seeking professional help for both the child and themselves can foster a nurturing environment that promotes growth, resilience, and understanding within the parent-child relationship.

Parenting a child with ADHD requires a delicate dance of compassion, discipline, and support. By embracing the challenges, seeking knowledge, and showing unwavering love for their child, parents can foster an environment that allows their child to thrive despite the hurdles posed by ADHD. Though the journey may be arduous, the rewards of a strong and resilient parent-child relationship can make it all worthwhile.

Chapter 3

"The Weight of Financial Strain: Navigating the Financial Costs"

The management of ADHD is not limited to emotional and behavioural challenges alone; it presents an additional financial burden that can weigh heavily on parents. The plethora of therapeutic interventions, medications, tutoring services, and other necessary measures can create a financial strain that adds to the complexities of raising a child with ADHD.

Addressing the multifaceted needs of a child with ADHD often requires a comprehensive approach, including a combination of therapies tailored to their specific challenges. Occupational therapy, for instance, may be recommended to develop crucial skills such as improved focus, self-regulation, and organizational abilities. However, the costs associated with these sessions can accumulate over time, putting strain on the financial resources of parents. From assessment fees to ongoing sessions, the expenses can mount and add financial stress to an already challenging situation.

In addition to therapeutic interventions, counselling can play a vital role in supporting both the child and the family in managing the demands of ADHD. The fees for counselling sessions can quickly become an additional financial burden, particularly if it is necessary to engage in regular or ongoing therapy to ensure the child's emotional well-being and to equip parents with effective coping strategies.

Pharmaceutical interventions, such as medication prescribed for ADHD, also contribute significantly to the financial costs. The recurring expenses for medications can stretch the financial stability of parents, especially when insurance coverage may be limited or non-existent. Moreover, finding the right medication and dosage often requires trial and error, leading to additional financial investments as different options are explored.

Education plays a pivotal role in the lives of children with ADHD, and additional academic support may be necessary to ensure their success. Tutoring sessions, specialized educational programs, or personalized education plans may be necessary to help ADHD children keep pace with their peers. However, these supplementary educational services can come with a hefty price tag, creating another layer of financial strain on parents.

Recognizing the importance of physical activity and its potential benefits in managing ADHD symptoms, athletic activities are often recommended. Whether it involves team sports or individual activities, the costs associated with enrollment, equipment, and membership fees might impose an additional financial burden on parents as they strive to provide their child with every opportunity to thrive.

The financial ramifications of supporting a child with ADHD can lead to significant strain for many parents. Some may be forced to make difficult decisions and sacrifices, compromising their own financial well-being and stability. Balancing the necessary expenses with other financial commitments can be a juggling act that contributes to added stress, anxiety, and financial pressure.

Society must acknowledge and understand the financial costs associated with managing ADHD. Increased awareness can help inspire support mechanisms and resources to alleviate the burden faced by parents. Government assistance programs, insurance coverage that recognizes the unique needs of children with ADHD, and community initiatives aimed at reducing financial barriers can all contribute to lightening the financial load on parents.

Navigating the complexities of ADHD management requires more than just emotional and behavioural support; it necessitates financial stability and access to resources. By understanding and addressing the financial strain experienced by parents, we can empower them to provide their children with the necessary tools and interventions, helping them thrive in both their academic and personal lives.

Chapter 4

"Understanding the Immense Commitment: Investing Time and Energy"

For many parents, the reality of managing their child's ADHD is an arduous journey that primarily relies on their unwavering commitment and dedication. When financial barriers obstruct access to specialized therapies, parents find themselves shouldering the primary responsibility of implementing coping strategies and behavioural interventions to navigate the daily challenges associated with ADHD. This involves crafting tailored routines, providing constant support, and employing innovative techniques to assist their child in thriving academically, socially, and emotionally.

Even for those fortunate enough to afford therapy, the journey towards ameliorating their child's condition is a ceaseless one. Endless quests for new treatments and remedies persist, leading to an incessant cycle of hope, anxiety, and exhaustion. The constant search for alternative therapies and innovative solutions to enhance their child's well-being often places a significant strain on parents' emotional and mental resilience.

The multifaceted struggle of nurturing a child with ADHD can swiftly become an overwhelming force in a parent's life. The relentless demands, combined with the emotional rollercoaster of witnessing their child navigate a world with ADHD, can lead to feelings of profound stress, isolation, and fatigue. The persistent quest to identify the most effective interventions and provide unwavering support can be an emotionally draining experience.

However, amid these challenges, the resilience, patience, and enduring love of parents emerge as crucial pillars in shaping a positive trajectory for their child. Despite the adversities, parental dedication and unwavering support serve as transformative forces, fostering an environment where children with ADHD can thrive and reach their full potential. With steadfast patience, unyielding love, and a strong support network, parents can create a nurturing environment that empowers their child to navigate the complexities of ADHD and lead a fulfilling life.

Chapter 5

"Unseen Struggles: the Profound Impact of ADHD on Siblings and Family Dynamics"

Living with a sibling who has ADHD presents a unique set of challenges that significantly affect the emotional landscape and development of the other child in the family. The second child often grapples with feelings of being sidelined or overlooked within the family dynamic. Parents' attention is naturally drawn towards the child with ADHD, given the demands and complexities associated with managing their condition. Consequently, the needs and emotions of the sibling can unintentionally take a back seat, fostering a sense of neglect and unmet expectations.

This situation places an immense emotional burden on the second child, who is frequently expected to comprehend and adapt to the circumstances without overt support or acknowledgment of their own emotional struggles. The inherent pressure to understand and cope can manifest in various distressing ways. Some siblings experience turbulent emotional swings, ranging from frustration to fits of anger or occasional spells of despondency, grappling with the unspoken complexities of their situation.

In certain cases, these unaddressed emotions can burgeon into a sense of resentment or animosity towards their sibling with ADHD. The desire for equitable attention from parents can spur behavioural patterns designed to garner the same level of care, resorting to actions such as feigning incompetence or purposefully acting out to attract notice. This unintended but fierce competition for parental attention intensifies the emotional strain on both the second child and the parent, leading to a complex web of strained relationships and heightened emotional stress.

The enduring impact of this sibling dynamic extends beyond childhood. It can significantly influence the emotional well-being and mental health of both the second child and the parent. The ongoing struggle to balance attention and support between the siblings can create a pervasive atmosphere of emotional distress within the family, impacting the overall harmony and stability of relationships.

Navigating this intricate dynamic requires a concerted effort from parents to acknowledge and address the emotional needs of both children. Creating an environment that fosters open communication, understanding, and equitable attention can play a pivotal role in alleviating the emotional strain experienced by the second child and fostering a more harmonious familial atmosphere.

Chapter 6

"The Isolation of Parenting a Child with ADHD: a Journey of Misunderstanding and Loneliness"

Raising a child with ADHD can be an incredibly challenging and emotionally draining experience for parents. Unfortunately, the journey is further compounded by the social isolation and heavy emotional burden they often face due to judgment and misunderstanding from friends, family, and even other parents.

Many parents of ADHD children find themselves avoiding family functions, feeling a constant sense of apprehension, fearing encountering name-calling and humiliation by ill-informed family members. They silently grapple with the reality that not everyone comprehends the intricacies and symptoms of ADHD, which further limits their ability to seek and find the essential support they so desperately need.

One of the most devastating consequences of this social isolation is the detriment to the parent's own mental and emotional well-being. With the vast majority of their attention and energy dedicated to navigating the challenges of their child's ADHD, these parents inadvertently neglect their own social lives, leaving little space for socializing and personal connections.

As they witness other parents gleefully boasting about their children's achievements, ADHD parents often find themselves feeling insecure, out of place, and overwhelmed with a sense of inadequacy. The relentless comparison and the constant reminders of their child's struggles can be deeply disheartening.

Perhaps one of the most heartbreaking aspects is observing their children's desperate attempts to fit in with their peers, only to be met with rejection or even bullying. This, further fuels the parents' inclination to withdraw from social interactions and shield themselves and their children from the potential pain of exclusion. The constant fear of their child being left out or mistreated can be an overwhelming burden to bear, leading parents to avoid most social gatherings altogether.

Consequently, the path of an ADHD parent can be exceedingly lonely and disheartening, as they navigate through a society that often fails to comprehend the unique challenges they face. The silent struggles they endure, shielding their child from judgment and advocating for their rights, deepen the divide between them and their support networks, leaving them feeling misunderstood and isolated.

It is crucial for society to recognize the profound impact that ADHD has on both the child and the parent, offering essential understanding, empathy, and support. By fostering an environment of compassion and education, we can alleviate the isolation that engulfs ADHD parents, providing a much-needed lifeline to a community that longs to feel seen, heard, and supported in their journey.

Chapter 7

"Navigating Challenges: Advocacy and Educational Hurdles"

The arduous nature of this advocacy role often manifests in a relentless pursuit to secure optimal educational provisions for the child. This endeavour involves a continuous cycle of advocacy, necessitating frequent interactions with teachers, school administrators, and educational specialists. Parents find themselves entrenched in a series of meetings, discussions, and correspondences, each aimed at ensuring that their child's unique needs are not only understood but also met effectively within the academic environment.

To fulfill the role of an effective advocate, parents need to delve deeply into comprehending their child's specific requirements and capabilities. This involves a comprehensive understanding of ADHD, its impact on learning and behaviour, and how it uniquely influences their child's educational experience. Armed with this knowledge, parents engage in collaborative partnerships with educators, aiming to tailor educational plans and strategies that cater to their child's individual needs.

Advocacy, in this context, extends beyond mere communication with school personnel. It involves actively participating in discussions regarding potential classroom modifications, interventions, and support mechanisms that could optimize the child's learning environment. Furthermore, parents navigate the complexities of addressing concerns about their child's progress, both academically and emotionally, ensuring that the support systems in place adequately cater to these multifaceted needs.

The multifaceted role of an advocate for a child with ADHD is undeniably challenging. However, amidst the challenges lie the seeds of profound reward and significance. By actively advocating for their child's needs, parents become instrumental in fostering an environment where their child not only copes but thrives. Each effort invested in these advocacy endeavours contributes significantly to ensuring that their child receives the necessary support to fulfill their potential and flourish academically and socially.

Therefore, to all parents navigating this intricate journey with a child having ADHD, your unwavering efforts and dedication as advocates do not go unnoticed. Your role as a pivotal advocate profoundly impacts your child's educational journey, ensuring they are equipped with the tools and resources needed to succeed. Your dedication serves as a beacon of hope, ensuring that every step taken in advocacy paves the way for your child's brighter future.

Chapter 8

"Untangling the Challenges: Self-care Struggles for Parents"

Parenting a child with ADHD constitutes a profound and consuming journey, demanding an extensive allocation of attention and effort. In the pursuit of ensuring their child's well-being and development, parents often inadvertently neglect their own physical, mental, and emotional health, leading to a cascade of adverse effects.

The perpetual responsibility of monitoring, supporting, and guiding a child with ADHD places a considerable strain on a parent's mental health. This strain tends to weigh particularly heavily on mothers, who may find themselves experiencing a spectrum of emotional challenges. Mood swings, intermittent feelings of anger, mounting frustration, and occasional bouts of depression become unwelcome companions as they grapple with the ceaseless demands of parenting a child with ADHD. The cumulative stress arising from perpetually juggling responsibilities can spiral into burnout, exacerbating anxiety, and contributing to a host of physical health concerns.

Amidst this whirlwind of parental responsibilities, it becomes imperative for caregivers to recognize the critical significance of self-care and prioritize it as a cornerstone of their routine. Cultivating a practice of self-care is not merely a luxury but a vital necessity to mitigate the detrimental effects of chronic stress and anxiety. Allocating time for oneself, regardless of its brevity, becomes a sanctuary where parents can recalibrate and rejuvenate. Engaging in simple yet rejuvenating activities such as taking a serene walk amidst nature, indulging in moments of reading for solace, or practicing mindfulness through meditation can serve as powerful antidotes to the overwhelming stress.

Furthermore, seeking support from friends, family, or mental health professionals is not a sign of weakness but an act of strength and self-awareness. Establishing a support network provides an invaluable outlet for emotional release, guidance, and reassurance, nurturing a sense of resilience and fortitude in facing the challenges associated with parenting a child with ADHD.

In summation, the journey of parenting a child with ADHD is undeniably multifaceted and demanding, requiring an intricate balance between caregiving and self-preservation. Recognizing the paramount importance of prioritizing personal well-being emerges as a fundamental pillar in ensuring that parents can offer the best possible care and support to their child. By embracing self-care practices and seeking the necessary support, parents can fortify themselves against the deleterious effects of chronic stress, thereby fostering a healthier and more nurturing environment for both themselves and their child.

Chapter 9

"Juggling Act: the Complexities of Balancing Work and Parenting"

Navigating the intricate balance between professional responsibilities and the demands of parenting is an intricate task faced by all parents. However, for parents of children grappling with ADHD, this balancing act is amplified, presenting a labyrinth of challenges that can lead to exhaustion and burnout.

The relentless necessity to cater to a child's unique needs while fulfilling professional commitments becomes an intricate dance, often leaving parents feeling physically and emotionally drained. In their pursuit to ensure their child receives adequate support, parents find themselves traversing a complex landscape filled with healthcare providers, therapists, and educators. This journey becomes notably arduous for parents new to the realm of ADHD, grappling with the complexities of understanding the condition and its far-reaching implications on their child's life.

Furthermore, the demands of raising a child with ADHD exert a palpable impact on parents' careers, often necessitating significant adjustments that can impact their professional trajectories. It's not uncommon for parents to take periodic leaves from work to attend to their child's pressing needs or meticulously rearrange their work schedules to accommodate therapy sessions and numerous appointments. For mothers, in particular, the decision to put their careers on hold or alter their work dynamics can become an agonizing dilemma. This adjustment may foster a sense of helplessness, prompting a reliance on others for support, while simultaneously inducing feelings of guilt and inadequacy for not being able to maintain the same level of professional commitment.

The emotional toll of making these sacrifices, coupled with the intricate balancing act between work and caregiving responsibilities, is a weighty burden for parents of children with ADHD. It presents an ongoing internal conflict, wherein the desire to provide unwavering support for their child's well-being collides with the aspirations and commitments within their professional spheres.

Yet, amidst these trials, parents find solace in the fulfillment derived from knowing they are actively supporting their child's journey toward success. Despite the tumultuous road, the unwavering dedication and sacrifices made by parents of children with ADHD become a testament to their resilience and unyielding love for their child's well-being.

This intricate balancing act, while laden with challenges, stands as a testament to the remarkable strength and commitment of parents who strive to ensure their child's success, fostering a future brimming with possibilities and achievements.

Chapter 10

"Thriving Through Adversity: the Resilient Journey of Parents Raising Children with ADHD"

The journey of parenting a child with Attention-Deficit/Hyperactivity Disorder (ADHD) is an intricate tapestry woven with challenges and adversities. However, within this intricate fabric of challenges lies a profound narrative of resilience, growth, and transformative experiences for parents.

Faced with the perpetual demands of supporting a child with ADHD, parents embark on an unforeseen path that demands unwavering resilience and adaptability. It's within the crucible of these challenges that parents cultivate a remarkable strength, evolving as individuals and as nurturers. Patience becomes their ally as they navigate through the daily hurdles, learning to embrace the ebb and flow of their child's unique needs with a newfound sense of understanding and fortitude.

In the crucible of parenting a child with ADHD, empathy emerges as a guiding light. Parents gradually develop an acute sensitivity to their child's struggles, fostering an empathetic connection that transcends the complexities of the condition. This empathy extends beyond the familial sphere, seeping into their interactions with others, cultivating a deeper understanding and compassion for individuals facing similar challenges.

Moreover, the constant problem-solving required in addressing the multifaceted needs of a child with ADHD acts as a crucible for refining their skills. Parents become adept problem solvers, navigating through a maze of therapeutic interventions, educational adaptations, and interpersonal dynamics. These acquired skills extend beyond the realm of parenting, laying the foundation for enhanced problem-solving abilities that can profoundly impact their personal and professional lives.

The resilience forged in the crucible of parenting a child with ADHD becomes a beacon of strength, propelling parents toward newfound opportunities and growth. Through determination and unwavering perseverance, they transform adversity into a source of inspiration, charting a path of personal growth and development.

Furthermore, this resilience is not merely confined to the realm of personal growth; it blossoms into a source of inspiration for others. Parents who navigate the labyrinth of challenges associated with ADHD serve as living embodiments of resilience, offering hope and encouragement to others facing similar journeys. Their experiences, shaped by determination and perseverance, stand as a testament to the power of resilience in surmounting seemingly insurmountable obstacles.

In essence, the journey of parenting a child with ADHD, although laden with challenges, becomes a transformative experience. Through resilience, adaptability, and an unwavering spirit, parents not only weather the storms but emerge as empowered individuals, wielding newfound skills and perspectives that illuminate pathways to growth and fulfillment.

As a parent navigating the complex terrain of raising a child with ADHD, establishing a robust support system becomes paramount. Seeking guidance from proficient professionals, including Paediatricians, Psychiatrists, or Therapists, serves as a foundational step. These experts provide invaluable assistance, starting with an accurate diagnosis, followed by personalized treatments and consistent monitoring to gauge progress.

In tandem with professional aid, connecting with fellow parents facing analogous challenges through support groups or online communities fosters a sense of solidarity and shared experiences. These platforms serve as havens for exchanging insights, seeking advice, and finding comfort in the understanding and empathy of others traversing a similar journey.

Recognizing the pivotal role of self-care in this intricate landscape is indispensable. Parents must acknowledge when they require assistance and actively seek support, whether from a partner, family member, or friend. Implementing self-care practices, such as regular exercise, mindfulness techniques like meditation, or indulging in hobbies, becomes a crucial cornerstone in managing stress and preserving a positive outlook amidst the trials of parenting a child with ADHD.

By nurturing a support network that blends professional guidance, communal understanding, and personal well-being, parents of children with ADHD can adeptly navigate the labyrinth of challenges while cherishing the joys inherent in parenting. This comprehensive approach, embracing professional aid, communal support, and prioritizing self-care, lays a robust foundation for families to thrive amidst the complexities of ADHD.

SECTION G

"EMPOWERING THE BOND BETWEEN PARENTS AND CHILDREN"

Raising a child with ADHD is a journey marked by unique trials and deeply rewarding moments. Yet, amidst this fulfilling path, parents often confront overwhelming challenges. Daily mood swings and frequent tantrums might become a perplexing labyrinth to navigate. Building a harmonious relationship with a child with ADHD is pivotal in averting constant conflicts and mitigating the need for raised voices or distressing confrontations.

Exploring the nuances of strengthening the parent-child relationship involves navigating a delicate yet rewarding path marked by understanding, resilience, and unwavering commitment. Here are pivotal steps for parents to fortify this bond:

Chapter 1

"Empowering Yourself with ADHD Knowledge: Enhancing Parenting and Supporting Your Child"

Understanding ADHD in detail is a cornerstone for parents. Each child's experience varies, so comprehending symptoms, treatments, and available medications is crucial. This knowledge fosters empathy and enables more effective symptom management.

Consider a simple scenario: Your child struggles to hold a spoon, leading to frequent spills while eating. Without understanding their impaired fine motor skills due to ADHD, reacting with frustration or criticism might occur. However, armed with knowledge about their condition, a different approach emerges—responding with empathy and patience.

Instead of reprimanding, encouraging their efforts and allowing them to learn through mistakes becomes key. Criticism or raised voices harm their self-esteem and elevate stress levels. Understanding their challenges paves the way for offering motivation and support, fostering improvement, and boosting their confidence.

Hence, delving into the intricacies of your child's challenges is pivotal. This understanding not only aids in better support and symptom management but also forges a stronger parent-child bond. Gathering detailed knowledge about ADHD equips you to navigate challenges effectively and foster an environment of understanding and encouragement.

Chapter 2

"Support Strategies: Nurturing Understanding and Patience"

ADHD presents challenges in focus, following instructions, and impulse control for children. It's crucial to grasp that children with ADHD don't intentionally misbehave; their brains function differently from those without the disorder. As a caregiver or parent, patience and empathy towards their struggles are paramount.

Repetition of instructions and visual aids can aid their focus and task retention. Frequent forgetfulness or misplacement of items is common; hence, establishing routines and designated spaces for belongings becomes essential. Additionally, unexpected emotional outbursts may arise, demanding a composed and patient response.

Understanding and accepting your child's behaviour is foundational. Working with their strengths and weaknesses facilitates success and nurtures self-esteem. Encouraging positive behaviour, implementing rewards, and fostering open communication foster a supportive atmosphere.

By blending patience, empathy, and structured approaches, you pave the way for your child with ADHD to flourish.

Chapter 3

"Supporting Stability: the Importance of Structure and Routine"

Children with ADHD often find it tough to navigate through unstructured environments. That's where a structured routine can make a world of difference, benefiting not just the child but the whole family. Picture this routine like a guiding map that helps reduce stress and confusion, allowing children to focus on their tasks better.

A consistent routine brings clarity by setting clear schedules and expectations. For kids with ADHD, this structured approach becomes a cornerstone for growth and independence. Predictable daily routines make adjusting to new situations easier, while constant changes can be overwhelming.

Yet, the benefits don't stop there. A structured routine is a lifeline for parents too. Juggling work, home, and a child with ADHD can be overwhelming. A set routine helps parents manage their day effectively and ensures their child's needs are met.

But here's the secret sauce: involving everyone in the family. When everyone chips in to manage the routine, appointments, and activities, the load doesn't fall solely on one parent. Sharing responsibilities helps keep things balanced. Consistency becomes the hero in managing ADHD, so aligning routines, rules, and consequences among family members is crucial. This harmony prevents confusion and mixed messages.

By establishing and involving the entire family in a structured routine, children with ADHD can flourish, paving the way for a happier, more successful journey ahead.

Chapter 4

"Effective Communication Strategies for Interacting with Children"

As a parent of a child with ADHD, keeping communication open and understanding is key. Encourage your child to express their feelings and worries while being there to listen actively and support them.

Children with ADHD often talk a lot, which can feel overwhelming. It's crucial not to dismiss their words as unimportant. This excessive talking is often how they express their thoughts and emotions. But sometimes, they might struggle to communicate effectively, leading to challenging behaviours like tantrums.

During these moments, it's essential to guide them in understanding and expressing their feelings. Don't brush off their emotions—help them recognize and handle what they're feeling. Teaching them how to manage their emotions will empower them to understand and control their behaviour better.

By instilling healthy communication skills, you're equipping them with vital tools for navigating life's challenges successfully. This supportive approach strengthens your connection with your child and helps them thrive.

Chapter 5

"Fostering Independence:
Tips and Strategies"

As parents, our goal is to guide our children toward independence and self-regulation. Sometimes, seeing them struggle might tempt us to do things for them. But stepping back and letting them tackle tasks, even if it's hard, is crucial for their growth.

Encouraging them to handle everyday activities like eating, dressing, packing bags, tidying up, and helping around the house builds their confidence. Slowly increasing responsibilities and allowing reasonable choices as they become more sure-footed empowers them.

Teaching self-reliance is vital. We won't always be by their side, so giving them the skills to handle life independently becomes our responsibility as parents. Encouraging independence today sets the foundation for their success tomorrow.

Chapter 6

"Family Collaboration: Strengthening Bonds While Managing Children's Needs"

When a child is diagnosed with ADHD, it's vital for the entire family to come together in understanding and supporting them. Yet, sometimes, siblings and grandparents might not get as much attention in this process.

Involving siblings is crucial, but it's equally important not to overlook their needs or burden them with responsibilities beyond their capacity. Parents should openly discuss ADHD with siblings, fostering a supportive atmosphere where everyone's feelings are heard and acknowledged.

For grandparents, educating them about ADHD is key. When they're aware of the condition and the household's structured routines, it helps prevent misunderstandings and conflicts within the family.

Each family has its unique dynamics, and what works for one might not for another. As kids grow and their needs change, family dynamics evolve too.

Being ready to adapt and adjust strategies is essential to accommodate these changes.

The cornerstone is maintaining a loving, supportive home environment while addressing the specific challenges of ADHD. Open communication and a united effort within the family can make a significant difference in managing the various dynamics that arise.

Chapter 7

"Modelling Behaviour: Being An Example for Your Child's Growth"

As a parent, your actions and behaviour serve as a blueprint for your child's learning. Modelling the conduct you wish to see in your child is crucial. This involves practicing good organization, effective time management, and self-control in your daily life. Managing your emotions well sets a positive example for your child to emulate.

Moreover, maintaining a routine, embracing healthy habits, and setting limits on screen time contribute to a healthy and cheerful home atmosphere for your child. Your child often mirrors your behaviour, so being disorganized, frustrated, or unable to manage emotions may lead them to adopt similar negative traits.

Building a peaceful home environment begins with modelling the behaviour you desire. Avoiding unregulated outbursts and instead showcasing positive behaviors and attitudes creates a conducive atmosphere for your child's growth.

Remember, the energy you put in is what you'll receive. By demonstrating the behaviours you hope to instill in your child, you pave the way for a content, resilient, and well-rounded child.

Chapter 8

"Prioritizing Well-being: The Importance of Self-care"

The journey of caring for a child with ADHD demands incredible resilience and patience. Yet, amidst this dedication, it's vital to prioritize your own well-being as a caregiver.

Taking care of your child at its best involves making time for self-care. This means carving out moments for yourself—whether it's a quiet coffee break, reconnecting with friends, nurturing your relationship with your partner, indulging in a spa day, or simply doing activities that bring you joy.

In the whirlwind of caregiving, it's essential to take breaks. Continuous dedication without pauses can lead to exhaustion, both physically and emotionally. A well-rested and emotionally nurtured parent is better equipped to support a child facing challenges related to ADHD.

Asking for help is not a weakness but a practical approach to self-care. Seeking support from family, friends, or support groups can ease the weight of caregiving responsibilities. Recognizing and addressing your own needs isn't selfish but a fundamental step that ultimately enhances the well-being of both caregiver and child in the long run.

Chapter 9

"Building Bonds: Meaningful Moments with Your Children"

Quality time is an essential aspect of building strong relationships, particularly with children who have ADHD. It involves being present and fully engaged during interactions and offering undivided attention during shared activities. Parents, at times, spend time with their children but are not involved. They may be in conversations with others, using screens, or processing their own thoughts.

While the duration of quality time matters, it's the quality of engagement that holds greater significance. Even short, focused sessions of quality interaction can have a more significant impact than extended periods of distracted attention. Regular, consistent quality time helps in building trust and connection over time. It doesn't have to be elaborate; even brief, daily moments count.

During quality time, it's essential to provide positive reinforcement and encouragement. Parents should acknowledge their children's efforts, strengths, and achievements to boost their confidence. It's important to steer clear of criticism or negative remarks during these moments and focus on creating a positive and supportive atmosphere.

Parents should be open to their child's preferences and adapt their activities accordingly. Flexibility allows for a more enjoyable and meaningful experience for both parent and child. Embracing spontaneity in activities often leads to the most memorable moments.

It's crucial to encourage activities that align with the child's interests. Whether it's playing a game, reading, drawing, or exploring nature, choosing activities that captivate the child's attention is vital. Parents often complain that they spend quality time with their child but they don't enjoy it. This is because the meaning of quality time may differ from parent to child. Therefore, it's important to do something that both the parent and the child can enjoy together.

Parents should be open to learning from their children. Their unique perspectives and experiences can offer valuable insights. Quality time doesn't necessarily mean engaging in extravagant activities; it's about fostering an environment of love, understanding, and connection. Tailoring these interactions to suit the child's interests and needs is crucial. Cherishing these moments as opportunities for growth and connection in the parent-child relationship can create a positive and lasting impact.

Raising a child with ADHD presents unique challenges, but a nurturing and supportive environment can make a significant difference. Strategies such as positive communication, clear boundaries, and positive reinforcement can help parents establish a strong and lasting bond with their children. Patience, dedication, and empathy are key to advocating for their child's well-being and growth. Ultimately, a supportive and loving environment can help children with ADHD overcome obstacles and thrive.

SECTION H

"UNCOVERING THE CHALLENGES: HOW SCHOOL AND EDUCATION CAN AFFECT CHILDREN WITH ADHD"

The impact of the school and education system on children with Attention-Deficit/Hyperactivity Disorder (ADHD) and their parents can be significant.

Chapter 1

Challenges in Focus and Attention

Children diagnosed with ADHD encounter persistent challenges in maintaining focus and attention, notably within the structured environment of a classroom. Their struggle to sustain attention spans can impede their capacity to comprehend instructions, complete assignments, and stay engaged with educational materials, significantly affecting their academic performance.

This difficulty often leads to situations where these children feel left behind or misunderstood. Teachers, while attempting to manage the classroom, might unintentionally single out students with ADHD, either through disciplinary actions or critical feedback. This unintended spotlighting further exacerbates feelings of self-doubt and contributes to a decline in their self-esteem.

As a consequence, these children may develop a sense of frustration, experiencing a continuous cycle of falling short of expectations and facing repercussions for factors beyond their immediate control. This ongoing struggle in the academic setting can significantly impact their confidence and willingness to engage in learning activities.

Chapter 2

Executive Functioning Skills

Children grappling with ADHD commonly encounter challenges in their executive functions, pivotal for vital skills like organization, time management, and planning. These struggles often manifest in missed assignments, inadequate time management, and a decline in academic performance.

The complexity of ADHD symptoms extends to daily routines, where children might grapple with frequent forgetfulness, and struggle to recall tasks or instructions, leading to misplaced items and disrupted routines. This forgetfulness can compound their struggles, causing frustration and impacting their ability to smoothly navigate daily activities.

Moreover, difficulties in organization can manifest in various ways, such as an inability to categorize or prioritize tasks, resulting in cluttered workspaces or difficulty breaking down assignments into manageable steps. Challenges with time management may lead to difficulties in estimating how much time a task will take, often resulting in delays or incomplete work.

These intricacies in executive functions profoundly impact a child's ability to function efficiently in academic and daily life settings, presenting ongoing hurdles that may necessitate targeted support and understanding from caregivers and educators.

Chapter 3

Peer Relationships

ADHD often face substantial social obstacles due to their impulsive and hyperactive tendencies. These challenges, stemming from difficulties in impulse control and sustaining attention, significantly impact their social interactions, friendships, self-esteem, and emotional well-being.

Their struggles with impulse control can lead to impulsive actions or comments, making it arduous for them to establish and retain friendships. Additionally, their tendency to be easily distracted and have difficulties maintaining focus can hinder their participation in group activities, leaving them feeling isolated and excluded.

Moreover, the manifestation of poor hand-eye coordination and attentional issues may further exacerbate their social experiences. These difficulties may hinder their ability to engage in team sports or cooperative activities, leading to feelings of inadequacy and social disconnection.

Unfortunately, these challenges might make children with ADHD susceptible to teasing or bullying from their peers. Their impulsive behaviour, which sometimes results in disruptions, can lead to further social alienation as it creates difficulties for others, thus perpetuating a cycle of social struggles.

Consequently, these social hurdles can significantly impact a child's sense of belonging and social confidence, emphasizing the importance of tailored support and understanding within social environments to promote inclusivity and emotional well-being.

Chapter 4

Stigmatization and Self-esteem

Children with ADHD often confront social stigma and misconceptions from both peers and educators, which can provoke profound emotional repercussions. The experience of being misunderstood or stigmatized might induce feelings of shame, embarrassment, and isolation among these children, significantly impacting their self-esteem and confidence.

These misconceptions and biases can lead to an environment where children with ADHD feel marginalized and less accepted by their peers. The challenges they face in academic and social settings might amplify these feelings, creating a sense of inadequacy and isolation, further eroding their self-perception and confidence.

Moreover, the struggles they encounter, such as difficulty concentrating or completing tasks, can foster a perception of being less capable compared to their peers. This discrepancy in performance might contribute to a sense of alienation and a belief in their own limitations.

In order to combat these detrimental effects, it's crucial for parents, teachers, and caregivers to recognize and comprehend the distinct challenges faced by children with ADHD. Providing tailored support, guidance, and encouragement becomes imperative in fostering an inclusive and supportive environment. Educating others about ADHD's complexities and advocating for empathy and understanding can go a long way in mitigating stigma and helping these children thrive academically and socially.

Chapter 5

Individualized Learning Needs

ADHD children often benefit from individualized or modified learning plans, such as an Individualized Education Program (IEP). These plans can help tailor educational approaches to their specific needs. Parents, teachers, special educators, therapists, and school coordinators are a part of IEP. They help develop a classroom-modified program to help the child cope with academics and the school environment.

A supportive and inclusive school environment can make a significant positive impact on both ADHD children and their parents. Here are some common classroom modifications for children with ADHD:

1. Effective classroom management for children with ADHD requires teachers to understand the condition and implement appropriate strategies.

2. Encouraging participation in various programs and building self-confidence is essential for the child's academic and social development.

3. A reward system that recognizes and praises positive behaviour and academic progress can also be implemented.

4. To help the child stay focused, it is recommended that they sit on the first bench and away from distractions such as doors and windows.

5. Reminders such as books, calendars, tiffin, and pencil boxes can be placed on the child's desk to help them stay organized and remember important items.

6. Teachers can also teach and reinforce organizational skills such as using a planner, keeping a tidy workspace, and using color-coded folders for different subjects.

7. Additional time can be provided for the child to gather and organize their materials, and instructions can be broken down into smaller, manageable steps.

8. Flexibility in assignments can be offered, allowing the child to demonstrate their knowledge in different ways such as oral presentations or projects.

9. Modified assignments can also be provided to match the child's skill level.

10. The use of noise-cancelling headphones.

11. Regular updates on the child's progress, challenges, and strategies for improvement can help parents and teachers work together effectively.

12. Creating an environment where ADHD is destigmatized and where all children are encouraged to embrace their differences can improve the overall school experience for children with ADHD.

13. It is important that teachers and school staff receive training on ADHD, its characteristics, and effective strategies for managing it.

14. Classroom modifications will vary based on the individual needs and strengths of each child with ADHD.

15. Regular communication and collaboration between teachers, parents, and any specialists involved in the child's care are essential for tailoring the best support strategies.

The educational experience of children with ADHD, along with the challenges faced by their parents, can significantly fluctuate based on the school's approach, the depth of teacher understanding, and the availability of supportive systems.

When schools provide the right support, a comprehensive understanding, and necessary accommodations, children with ADHD can flourish in their educational endeavours. Simultaneously, parents can navigate the complexities of raising a child with ADHD more effectively when they receive adequate support.

Ultimately, the collaboration between educators, support staff, and parents in implementing suitable strategies and accommodations plays a pivotal role in fostering an environment where children with ADHD can thrive academically and socially.

SECTION I

"UNLOCKING HARMONY: PROVEN STRATEGIES FOR MANAGING BEHAVIOUR IN CHILDREN WITH ADHD"

Navigating the unique challenges of parenting a child with ADHD requires patience, understanding, and a tailored approach to managing their behaviour. Attention Deficit Hyperactivity Disorder (ADHD) often presents itself as a complex puzzle, influencing various facets of a child's life, including their behaviour. In this article, we'll explore effective strategies and techniques that can assist parents and caregivers in supporting children with ADHD, empowering them to navigate and manage behavioural patterns with compassion and practicality. Understanding the nuances of ADHD behaviour and implementing targeted approaches can make a profound difference in a child's life and family dynamics. Let's delve into a comprehensive guide on managing behaviour in children with ADHD.

Chapter 1

"Mastering the Art of Following Structured Instructions"

It's important to remember that you can't give detailed instructions all at once. Doing so will result in having to repeat the same instructions several times, which can be frustrating in the end. For example, if you want your child to complete a bedtime routine that involves brushing, washing their face, changing into their night clothes, and going to bed, you can't give them all of these instructions at once. Instead, you should tell them each step one at a time. After a few days of practicing this routine, they will learn the pattern and you won't have to repeat everything.

Another helpful tip is to start naming all of the daily routines. For instance, the bedtime routine includes brushing teeth, washing the face, changing into night clothes, and going to bed. By naming each routine, your child will know exactly what to do after practicing it several times. Here are some examples of daily routines I use in my daily life:

- **Morning routine:** using the washroom, brushing teeth, washing face, and changing into uniform

- **Breakfast routine:** having water, honey with turmeric, eating breakfast, and cleaning up afterward
- **Bus routine:** wearing shoes, carrying a bag and bottle, opening the door, and calling the lift
- **Afternoon routine:** removing shoes, putting bag and bottle away, taking a shower, changing clothes, and putting dirty clothes in the laundry bag
- **Snacks routine:** having water, eating snacks, and cleaning up afterward
- **Classes routine:** checking bag, carrying bottle, wearing shoes, opening the door, and calling the lift
- **Dinner routine:** washing hands, having water, eating dinner, and cleaning up afterward
- **Bedtime routine:** using the washroom, brushing teeth, washing face, changing into night clothes, and going to bed

It's important to give your child instructions one at a time and to be consistent with your reminders. Even if your child makes mistakes, don't give up on them. Keep reminding them and make sure they do it themselves. Don't let any house help or siblings do their work for them. Your job as a parent is to teach them to be self-reliant. Remember that this process takes time and patience, but it's worth it in the end.

"From Small Wins to Big Victories: the Power of Positive Reinforcement in Building Good Habits"

Positive reinforcement is a powerful tool involving the conditioning of the mind through affirmative feedback. Encouraging your child, no matter the scale of their efforts, is crucial in fostering progress. Even small steps should be acknowledged, as they pave the way for greater achievements. For instance, if your child masters two-letter words, express appreciation; this motivates them to tackle more complex three-letter words.

Be specific in your praise to guide their focus towards areas of improvement. Acknowledging their ability to write on the blue line without touching the red line, for instance, highlights their accomplishment precisely. Specific feedback enables your child to recognize their progress and understand where they can improve further.

When you celebrate even the smallest advancement, your child feels valued and acknowledged, fueling their motivation to seek your attention and appreciation again. This reinforcement methodology nurtures a continuous cycle of improvement.

Implementing positive reinforcement is particularly beneficial for children with ADHD. Offering specific praise for their effort, progress, and task completion helps bolster their motivation and confidence in their capabilities.

Chapter 3

"Overcoming Disappointment: Strategies for Coping and Moving Forward"

Dealing with disappointment is a personal challenge that both you and your child will face. Discouragement can take place at any stage and accepting it and working on it is crucial. It's important to refrain from getting upset or denying any discouragement that your child faces. Keep in mind that your reaction to every situation has a significant impact on your child.

For instance, when my son was in the first grade, his reading teacher would scold him for his inability to read five-letter words that other kids could read effortlessly. My son used to come home upset and complain that he didn't like his teacher because she would always shout. I explained to him that his teacher was merely doing her job, which was to ensure that every child could read seven-letter words before reaching second grade. I assured him that she wasn't a bad person but perhaps her way of communicating wasn't correct. I also advised him to continue working on his reading, and that I would talk to his teacher. I reminded him that he was improving and that I was proud of him. He had started reading from scratch, and now he could read three-letter words, I was confident that he could read five-letter words as well if he didn't give up. I made him believe in himself and assured him that I always loved and supported him.

These words changed his attitude towards reading and his teacher. Instead of complaining and getting discouraged, he came home and said, "Mom, the teacher said I could not read seven-letter words, and she was upset, but I did read three and four-letter words, so I know I am doing better." He was delighted and proud of his progress.

By explaining his teacher's role, I made him more positive towards her. Blaming the teacher and agreeing with the child can make them lose respect for their teachers and refuse to take responsibility for their actions. Secondly, I made him understand that he had a drawback, which was his inability to read five-letter words, but he could read three-letter words, which was a success. Both these messages were conveyed positively and encouragingly. Lastly, I made him believe in himself that he could read better and improve. When you accept your child with all their flaws and avoid judging or comparing them, it's a big achievement for both of you.

Chapter 4

"Fun and Productive: Tips for Planning Your Day with Children"

Regulating emotional breakdowns can be challenging for children with ADHD. It's important to avoid triggering them with unplanned decisions. You can work with your child to create a checklist of daily tasks such as chores, bathing, meals, screen time, school work, playtime, and sleep patterns.

To make things easier, create a planner and place it where it can be easily accessed, like on a cupboard. Communicate with your child a day in advance to prepare them for the following day. This can even be planned for outings. For instance, if you plan to go shopping, talk to your child a day before and make a list of items that need to be purchased. Ask your child what they would like to buy, like stationary, clothes, or a particular toy, and discuss the reasons why they want those things. After validating all options, agree on one item that you will buy for them. This way, they will not throw tantrums or create drama when you go shopping.

I always use this concept. Whenever we decide to go shopping, we make a list together. We even discussed how much money we could spend and agreed to follow the list and budget. When we go shopping, it becomes easier because we have already decided on what can be purchased. If my son likes anything and needs it, he will tell me to write it down in the next shopping list. It becomes easy and hassle-free. I use this concept every time, even for dinners, play zones, or movies, and it works wonders.

Once everything is planned with your child, you both will enjoy your trips together without any stress. You can use this approach every time you plan to go out of the house, whether it's a movie or a family outing. Decide what time to start getting ready, what time to leave, and what to buy during the interval, if necessary. This way, your child will always be prepared, and there will be no room for drama or tantrums.

Remember, children are not difficult to manage. They just need to know what to expect. By planning with your child, you can make things easier and more enjoyable for both of you.

Chapter 5

"Effective Strategies for Handling Unexpected Situations with Children"

As a parent, it's natural to want things to go as planned, but sometimes life throws us curveballs. When things don't go as expected, it can be frustrating and overwhelming, especially when dealing with children who may react with anger, crying, or misbehaviour. However, it's important to remember that these are just temporary phases and can be dealt with in a composed manner.

One of the first things to keep in mind when dealing with such situations is to ensure that your tone is acceptable and not loud. Yelling or scolding your child may only make the situation worse. Instead, try to communicate with them and understand what's bothering them. Avoid using the word 'no' as it might make them more rebellious. For instance, you can say something like, "I can hear you. You seem to be upset. Could you help me understand what's making you so upset?" or "I understand you're angry but is shouting helping you? Could you talk to me so we can find a solution to this?"

I remember an incident when we had plans to go out, but it got cancelled due to some work commitments. My son was very upset. He started throwing things, yelling, and crying. I requested him to please not throw things, but he did it more. It was his way of showing he was upset and rebelling against what I said. I stayed calm for some time and let him remove his anger. Then I softly told him, "I understand you are angry and upset that we are not going out. Even Mamma wanted to go out, but instead, she had to work. Can you imagine how bad I am feeling?" Then he calmed down because I gave him something to ponder. I continued, "Can you come here, and we can talk and find a solution where you and Mamma both can be happy?" He looked at me, paused, and slowly sat down. But he did not come to me. I went up to him and told him, "Can you give a hug to Mamma? I will feel better." Then we hugged each other. I could feel his pulse calming down, and then he burst into crying. I hugged him tight and told him, "I understand you are feeling sad, but it's not the end, right? We can always plan again on another day. Today, I will finish my work, and we can plan a movie date. Imagine, at least you can still play around, but Mamma has to work. And if you don't support me, how will I manage? You are my strength. We both have to help each other, right? We are a team?" And he looked at me and said, "But mamma, I really wanted to go today. I told all my friends." I replied, assuring him we would make a plan again, and today we have a choice to make a new plan instead of spoiling the day by getting angry and crying. He mellowed down, and everything went well. Imagine if I would have shouted at him, punished him, sent him to his room, or been ignorant of his feelings. It would have made him feel unwanted and unheard. It's important to realize that the actions of your child are mere expressions of resentment and have to be dealt with love and understanding. They don't do this to disrespect you or hurt you; they do it because they feel unloved. When you react with yelling and hitting, it makes their feelings stronger as you validate that you don't love them. Instead, show them love, care, and understanding, and clear their doubts. They will respond with the same love and care to you.

When you communicate with your child in a way that shows you want to hear and understand them, they'll be more likely to listen to you. It's important to be patient and consistent in your approach., but don't give up on your child. Keep trying until you find the solution that works for both of you.

It's also important to remember that children often look to their parents for guidance on how to handle difficult situations. By modelling calm and composed behaviour, you can help your child learn how to manage their emotions and deal with unexpected situations in a healthy way.

In summary, when things don't go as planned, it's important to keep your cool and communicate with your child in a way that shows you want to hear and understand them. Be patient, and consistent, and model calm behaviour to help your child learn how to manage their emotions and deal with unexpected situations in a healthy way.

Chapter 6

"Empowering Children: Why Mothers Should Guide, Not Control"

As mothers, we often tend to micromanage every aspect of our children's lives. From what they eat to what they wear, when they sleep, and even when they need to use the washroom, we try to control everything out of concern for their well-being. However, in doing so, we may end up hindering their growth and development, making them overly dependent on us for even the smallest of decisions.

As parents, it is our foremost duty to guide our children and help them develop into independent individuals who can make their own decisions. It is important to find a balance between providing guidance and allowing them to make their own choices. For instance, instead of dictating what they should wear, we can suggest that they wear a full-sleeved shirt since it might be cold in the theatre. We can then let them decide what they want to wear. Even if we think they have made the wrong decision, we should not impose our thoughts on them. It is important for them to face the consequences of their actions and learn from their mistakes. Sometimes, mothers tend to protect their children from facing consequences. However, this protection can become suffocating for the child. It is important to let them learn by trial and error and realize the significance of rational thinking and decision-making rather than being too stubborn with their ideology. Similarly, instead of telling them when to use the washroom, we can explain the situation and let them make their own decision. For example, we can say that we will be on the road for two hours, and there won't be any washrooms on the way. It might be a good idea to use the washroom now. By doing so, we empower our children to think for themselves and take control of their lives.

Encouraging our children to make their own decisions and trusting their choices can help them develop a sense of freedom and confidence. It can also foster a healthy parent-child relationship based on mutual respect and trust. So, let's guide our children, not control them, and help them become independent and responsible individuals.

Chapter 7

"Raising Confident Children: The Importance of Realistic Expectations"

I can understand the struggles that parents face while raising an ADHD child.

It's a common scenario where parents feel intense pressure from schools and society to have their child compete and be perfect. However, it's crucial to take things slow and make your own choices. Putting too much pressure on your child can be overwhelming for both of you, leading to frustration and a lack of progress.

Therefore, it's advisable to write down your goals and focus on your child's abilities and progress. For instance, when my child was in 1st grade, he struggled to read seven-letter words while his peers could. Instead of feeling the pressure, I refused to let it get to me. I focused on his progress, set small goals for him to achieve, and encouraged him along the way. Today, my son can read storybooks independently and takes pride in his progress.

It's essential to remember not to fall into unrealistic expectations from school, family, or society. As a parent, you know your child best, so set small goals, achieve them, and celebrate your child's progress. Life will become much easier, and your child will thrive under your supportive care.

Chapter 8

"Empowering Parents of Children with ADHD and LD: Celebrating Strengths and Overcoming Challenges"

As a parent, it can be overwhelming to learn that your child is being assessed for ADHD or LD. It's common to feel like you need to hide this information from others, fearing that your child will be cornered or not accepted. However, it's important to remember that acceptance starts with you. If you can accept your child's diagnosis without any doubts or insecurities, the world will follow suit.

It's important to recognize that children with ADHD are often highly intellectual and possess unique strengths that may not be immediately apparent. For example, your child may struggle with attention, reading, writing, and everyday tasks that other children find easy, but they may excel in other areas, such as math or problem-solving. It's essential to celebrate these strengths and not let the challenges overshadow them.

It's also important to understand that the challenges your child faces are not insurmountable.

With proper guidance and nurturing, they can overcome these obstacles and thrive. For example, your child's teacher may be able to make classroom modifications to help them stay focused, such as seating them at the front of the class or providing reminder notes on their desk.

Collaborating with teachers and professionals involved in your child's care, such as paediatricians, therapists, or school counsellors, is crucial. By maintaining open communication with these individuals, you can develop strategies and interventions that support your child's needs both at home and at school. This collaboration can also help teachers better understand your child's strengths and challenges, allowing them to provide more effective support.

Finally, don't hesitate to ask for help. Informing a few parent friends in the same class who can help with everyday notes or seeking guidance from professionals can make a significant difference in your child's success. Remember, with patience, understanding, and support, your child can thrive and reach their full potential.

Chapter 9

"Creating a Non-distracting Environment for Your Child's Homework: Tips for Parents"

As parents, we often expect our children to concentrate and finish their homework or tasks on time, but we fail to provide them with a non-distracting environment. With family members talking in loud voices, the television on, the maid working, and some moms continuing their work on their phones while sitting next to their children, it becomes challenging for a child to focus and complete their work.

To help your child concentrate better, it is essential to create an environment that minimizes distractions. You can start by reducing noise, clutter, and visual stimuli as much as possible. Designate a quiet, well-organized study area that is free from distractions to help your child concentrate better during homework or other tasks.

You can also use timers to structure time and help with transitions between activities. When you sit with your child to make them study, make sure there is no one else around. Set a time limit for a worksheet to complete, decide on an activity to be done in break time, and then get back to studies. Avoid using your phone or any other distractions while you are with your child.

This way, you are aware of how much time you need to dedicate to your child, and you are sure that it will be done in that time. Instead of sitting all day, distracted, yelling, and not getting things done, keep an hour aside, dedicated to your child, structure it, and the tasks are done. This approach works wonders and helps your child concentrate better, leading to better academic performance.

Chapter 10

"Letting Children Grow: Why It's Important to Let Things Happen in Their Own Time"

As a parent, it's natural to want the best for your child and to help them overcome any challenges they may face. However, it's important to remember that not everything needs to be fixed right away. Sometimes, it's best to let things happen in their own time.

For example, when my son was around 3 years old, he had a fear of rain. He would refuse to leave the house if he saw dark clouds in the sky, and it was a struggle to get him to go to school or play outside during rainy weather. Many people around me suggested that there was a problem with him and that it needed to be fixed. However, I saw it as just a phase and didn't want to force him to change his perception of rain.

Instead, I encouraged him to play with water in other ways. He loved water games and playing in the pool, so I knew that he didn't have a fear of water in general. I didn't overthink or worry about his fear of rain, and eventually, he grew out of it on his own. Now, at 7 years old, he can't wait for the rainy season to arrive so he can jump in puddles and get drenched in the rain.

Similarly, my son didn't show much interest in arts and crafts when he was younger. Many people suggested that art was a great therapy and that I should encourage him to do it more often. However, I didn't want to force him into something he didn't enjoy. Instead, I gave him paper and colours and let him scribble or do whatever he wanted. Sometimes he would make pieces of paper and throw them away, and other times he would draw something that I couldn't quite understand.

But I didn't compare him to other kids his age who were better at art, and I didn't try to force him to be something he wasn't. I let him explore his interests and strengths, and eventually, he started showing more interest in drawing. Now, he asks me for a piece of paper to draw on and his drawings are more complex and detailed than before.

The lesson here is that every child has their limitations and strengths, and it's important to work with them accordingly. Don't try to fix everything right away, and don't compare your child to others. Let them grow and develop in their own time, and you may be surprised at how much they can achieve.

Chapter 11

"Embracing Your Child's Uniqueness: Overcoming Comparisons as a Parent of a Child with Special Needs"

As a parent, you may have heard it multiple times before, but it's important to acknowledge that subconsciously, parents do compare their children. Phrases such as "other kids of his age don't behave this way" or "I know my child is lacking, but when will he catch up?" are nothing less than comparisons. These doubts arise because you are subconsciously comparing your child with others, and hence are worried about their developmental growth.

It's important to understand that every small improvement in your child is growth. Take it slow. While it can be difficult to see your child struggle, it's important to accept and embrace it. Kids with special needs are called "special" because they possess a unique quality. Yes, they may lack in some things, but they excel in something else. You just need to find it encourage your child, and give them the platform to succeed.

For instance, my son is incredible at maths. When his class was still learning 2-digit addition and subtraction, he was doing 3-digit sums and knew tables from 1 to 10. Although he struggled with writing, we practiced every day, and because he loved maths, he improved drastically. Every child has a unique ability, whether it is in sports, spelling, or numbers. You just need to explore and encourage your child's talents.

Remember that your child may be lacking in some areas, but they are also capable of many things. You just need to be their guiding light.

"Helping Kids Manage Their Emotions: Strategies for Dealing with Extreme Feelings"

As a mother, you may experience extreme levels of emotions and wonder where you went wrong. But it's normal to feel this way. Mothers often use guilt as a tool when things go wrong. To guide your child to manage their emotions, you need to manage your emotions well. When there are extreme levels of emotions, keep calm. Take deep breaths and remind yourself that it's just a phase. You need to deal with the problem your child is facing, not your child.

It's important to understand that your child is not creating problems for you. They are in a problem and need your guidance to deal with it. Once you realize that it's you and your child against the problem, not you against your child, you can control the way you react.

You need to explain this same equation to your child. When you tell them to stop, calm down, and be quiet, it's not helping them at all. They feel that you are stopping them from expressing themselves and not understanding them. Instead, try hugging them and telling them that it's okay to cry or get angry. Let them be themselves in your presence because you are their safe place.

If your child is reluctant to touch and does not want to hug, make eye contact and tell them the same thing. Show this with your body language as well. Don't worry about what other people are thinking, only worry about your child and look at them.

Once your child has vented out, calmly tell them to go home if you are out. If you are home, you can stay where you are or move to another room. The reason to move is to take your child away from the situation that is triggering them at that point.

Next, ask them if they want to tell you what is troubling them. If they agree, listen to them carefully. There are many underlying explanations for spoken and unspoken words. Don't interrupt them while they are speaking. Let them complete their sentences.

I'll give you an example. One day, my son came home crying, howling, and rolling on the floor. I didn't know what was wrong, whether he fell or got hurt. So, I went to him and asked if he wanted to talk about it. He just cried even louder. I stayed with him and told him that I was there for him whenever he was ready to talk. After a while, he calmed down and hugged me. I observed him and found out that his favourite bottle was broken. I didn't say anything and just hugged him back.

Later, he told me that he would never talk to his friend because he fought with him and broke his favourite bottle. I didn't give him any advice at that moment because I knew he was upset about his bottle. Instead, we went to his room, freshened up, and changed. He had dinner, and we played a game. Before going to bed, I shared my experience with him.

I told him that I lost my favourite bag in a cab, and I cried a lot just like him. The next day, I got a new bag. I explained to him that nothing stays forever and that he should take care of his belongings. If something is lost or broken, crying won't bring it back. He needs to get a new one. Maybe he won't get the same thing, but he can always find something good, and that can become his next favourite. So, he understood that he was upset that his friend broke his bottle, but he couldn't have it fixed. We will buy a new bottle tomorrow, and he needs to take care of it.

He hugged me, kissed me, and said thank you, mamma. He went off to sleep with a smile. Remember, when your child is having a flush of emotions, trying to stop or explain at that moment will never help but will make things worse. You will end up shouting or hitting, and your child will lose trust in you. You are the safe place for your child. Don't let anything or anyone change that.

Chapter 13

"Prioritizing Nutritious Food: A Key Component for Maintaining Good Health and Well-being"

As a concerned mother, I was advised to limit my child's intake of chocolates, biscuits, wafers, and junk food to only Sundays. However, I soon realized that completely depriving my child of these foods was not the best approach. I explained to him the negative effects of consuming too much junk food and we agreed to limit his intake to a moderate amount.

I allowed him to have a few plain biscuits in his tiffin and a chocolate cookie, chips, or a bar of chocolate after he ate a whole fruit. I made sure he did not consume any junk food after 5 pm and only after he had eaten something healthy. This way, he was able to enjoy his favourite foods in moderation and was mindful of his eating habits.

I learned that depriving a child of their favourite foods can lead to behavioural issues and feelings of being underprivileged. It's important to find a balance and teach them to make healthy choices while still allowing them to enjoy their childhood.

"Boost Your Child's Brain Development with Fun and Engaging Brain Exercises"

Engaging in brain exercises can significantly contribute to the development of your child's brain. It is crucial to encourage your child to participate in brain-boosting exercises daily. Such exercises can aid in enhancing focus and attention. Brain exercises for children are primarily focused on hand-eye coordination and are often performed with the help of hands. Brain gym toys and activities are readily available in the market, which can be utilized to make brain exercises more enjoyable for children.

You can purchase puzzles, memory games, and creative thinking games to engage your child in brain exercises. However, it is important to ensure that your child doesn't feel pressured or overwhelmed while performing these exercises. If your child finds the exercise too challenging, he might not be interested in continuing it, and he might give up. To avoid this situation, you should try to make the exercise more fun and engaging for your child. You can motivate him and encourage him to participate in the exercises with you. Remember, you should never give up on your child, and you should always stay with him and try to make it a fun play.

Chapter 15

"Breaking the Silence: the Struggle of Overcoming Parental Stigma"

As a parent, it can be challenging to understand the behaviour of children who have ADHD and LD. Unfortunately, some parents advise their children to avoid interacting with ADHD and LD children, believing that it is essential for their kids to only be around well-behaved and intellectually advanced children. However, it is crucial to break this stereotype and redefine the meaning of "good" company for children.

A "good" company is not necessarily a group of intellectually advanced kids, but rather a group of emotionally available friends who stand by and support your child. Children with ADHD are emotionally sensitive and available, and they are well-behaved and aware of others' behaviours. Although they may struggle with certain tasks, they are undoubtedly intelligent.

If you encounter a parent who draws a line between their child and yours, do not take it personally. It may be a result of their lack of knowledge about ADHD.

As a parent, you should not stop sending your child to social gatherings or birthday parties. Instead, take the opportunity to meet new people and help them understand your child's behaviour. When they observe your child, they will realize that they have formed the wrong impression about children with ADHD.

I used to accompany my child to parties and ask the parents if I could stay as my child might struggle on his own. Sometimes we weren't invited to parties, but I never took it personally. I was happy that my child had a small but meaningful circle of friends who accepted him for who he was. I didn't want him to get lost in the crowd. I am proud that my son is now invited to parties and play dates, and parents tell me that they want their child to be friends with my son because he is emotionally available, understanding, and caring. They don't believe he has ADHD or any other problem. This is the magic of raising emotionally healthy children.

"Effective Ways to Help Your Child Cope with Peer Problems"

Just like parents, some children also fail to understand kids with ADHD. Your child may feel excluded in games as they may miss instructions or have difficulty playing due to their weak motor skills. Other kids may tease and bully them, causing your child to feel left out, cry, and become isolated. I have personally witnessed this every week in school, in the building, and in classes where my child was bullied and left out. He wasn't allowed to play with other kids, and he often had lunch alone. It broke my heart to see him fight his loneliness and try so hard for others to accept him. However, I never stopped him from going out to play. Instead, I encouraged him to be himself and find a way to cope. I told him that it's great to have friends around, but if no one wants to be around you someday, don't feel bad. Learn to love your own company. Only if you love yourself will others love you, and only if you accept yourself will others accept you. So, if someone doesn't want to play or share lunch, enjoy your own company. Don't let anyone else decide your worth. You should always be happy and never let others make you feel sad. I kept reminding him of this every time he felt left out, and it immediately made him feel better. One day, he came home from school very happy. When I asked him why he was so happy, he said, "Mom, I remember you told me to enjoy my company, and that's what I did. I was alone, enjoying myself, and thinking about you, and it made me feel better." This brought tears to my eyes, but I held strong and hugged him, telling him how proud I was of him and how much I loved him. We need to understand that our kids will face challenges in every area of life, and we won't always be there to help them. Therefore, it is essential to make them emotionally strong by showing them what strength is.

"Unlocking the Potential of Children with ADHD: How to Make Learning Fun and Engaging"

When it comes to children with ADHD, it's not uncommon for them to struggle with studying and focusing on their schoolwork. It can be challenging for them to pay attention, read, write, and engage in any learning activity that requires a great deal of concentration. As a parent, you must approach this situation with understanding and patience. Instead of being strict or resorting to shouting or hitting, try to make studying fun for your child.

Your job isn't just to ensure that your child finishes their homework, but also to make the learning process enjoyable for them so that they don't develop a negative attitude towards studies. You can do this by allowing your child to select the subject they want to study on days when they're feeling less motivated. Ask them if they want to read, write, do English, do maths, draw, colour, or make patterns, as everything is a learning experience for them. Engaging in these activities can help improve their finger grip, focus, and hand-eye coordination.

When studying with your child, keep in mind that they may not be able to sit still for too long. Therefore, you must set a time limit and give them breaks of 5 minutes in between. During these breaks, let your child walk, run, or jump around, as it can help them release built-up energy and improve their focus when they return to their study session. By creating a positive and engaging learning environment, you can help your child with ADHD to excel academically while also enjoying the process.

"Simple Tips to Start a Meaningful Conversation with Your Child"

As a firm believer in the importance of emotional independence for children, I have always emphasized the need for them to understand their emotions and learn how to regulate them effectively. However, I have noticed that when parents discover that their child has ADHD or LD, they tend to shift their focus to academic performance and physical activity, neglecting the child's emotional well-being.

To address this issue, I suggest that parents should try to focus on their child's feelings and thoughts, as their behaviour is a reflection of their emotions. When your child comes home from school, instead of asking them if they completed their work, try asking them who they shared their lunch with or what made them happy that day. By asking open-ended questions that encourage your child to reflect on their emotions and experiences, you can help them better understand and manage their feelings.

This approach also shows your child that you care about more than just their academic performance, which can boost their self-confidence and sense of security. It helps them feel valued and understood, which can enhance their way of thinking and validating their feelings.

It's important to avoid asking close-ended questions that only require one-word answers, such as "how was your day?", "Did you finish your lunch?" or "Is there any homework?" Instead, ask questions that allow your child to share their thoughts and feelings, such as "What was the best part of your day?" or "Tell me about your favourite class today." By doing so, you can gain a better understanding of your child's experiences and emotions, which can help you manage their behaviour more effectively.

Chapter 19

"Letting Kids Make a Mess: Why It's Important to Prioritize Exploration Over a Perfectly Clean Home"

As parents, we all want our homes to be clean and tidy. However, as much as we try, children can make a mess from time to time. It's important to remember that kids learn through exploration, and this means that they need the freedom to play and make a mess. Even if your child has ADHD and struggles with impulse control, they still need to explore and learn in their way. It's crucial not to stifle their curiosity and creativity.

If you're always cleaning up after your child, you'll end up spending all your time doing so. On the other hand, if you only allow your child to play with one thing at a time, they might get bored and start playing with things they're not supposed to, which could lead to more messes or even damaged items.

So, what should you do? First of all, it's essential to accept that a messy house is okay. Your home won't be untidy forever, and you can manage for a few years.

There will be times when your child may not only play with toys but also with the furniture in your home. For instance, my son has broken multiple cupboards, torn sofa sets, and even the base of dining chairs. He has thrown a bat at the TV and hurled various items outside the balcony. Our house was filled with broken furniture, torn sofas, and a TV with a significant crack for two years.

Initially, my husband wanted to renovate and replace everything, but I managed to convince him that every new item we got would be damaged in a few days due to our son's hyperactivity. We couldn't afford to spend our energy taking care of things; we needed it to take care of our son. Our primary goal was not to impress guests, and most of the time, we avoided inviting them over. Although there were times when our house was a mess, I would politely apologize and explain that my son liked to play that way. I couldn't keep cleaning all the time because I had other chores to attend to. I wasn't trying to please anyone but rather focused on how much energy I had and what I could do.

In conclusion, it is crucial to let your child play and explore without worrying too much about the mess. A little bit of mess is okay, and it won't last forever. It's important to prioritize your child's needs and well-being over a perfectly clean home. Remember, you don't have to impress anyone with a spotless house, and it's okay to set boundaries and communicate them politely to your guests.

"Organization is Key: Tips for Creating a Tidy and Entertaining Toy Space for Children"

Teaching your child, the value of organization and cleanliness is crucial to help them develop good habits that will help them throughout their lives. When it comes to organizing your child's toys, making different boxes for different types of games can be very helpful. It's important to note that these boxes should contain multiple toys, not just one.

For example, you can create a construction box that includes Lego, building blocks, and magnetic tiles. You can also create a sensory play box that includes clay, sand play, slime, and moulds, and similarly, you can have puzzle boxes, role play sets, arts and crafts sets, car sets, and more. By letting your child choose the box he wants to play with and removing one box at a time, you can keep your child entertained for hours.

As your child plays, encourage him to use his creativity, explore, think outside the box, and brainstorm new ideas. The best thing about these boxes is that since everything is in one place, your child can easily keep the toys back inside by himself, and you don't need to worry about organizing them.

To keep your home organized, it is helpful to use different shelves or boxes for clothes based on their category, such as uniforms, socks, nightwear, home clothes, and outdoor clothes. Similarly, you can have separate shelves for school books, home practice books, and reading books.

When my son turned six, I started keeping different labelled boxes for him. This made it easy for him to locate his things and put them back in the right place. Before he turned six and was unable to take responsibility, however, my house was always messy. It takes time, effort, and patience to teach children to be organized, and consistency is key. By following these tips, you can make your child's life easier and keep your home tidy and organized.

Chapter 21

"How to Handle Clingy Behaviour in Children: a Parent's Guide to Encouraging Independence and Fostering Self-reliance"

It is a common phenomenon to observe clinginess in children towards their mothers, regardless of their age, and it is indicative of the child's need for security, comfort, and attachment. While the manifestation of this behaviour may differ based on the child's age and personality, the primary motive remains the same - seeking reassurance and safety from their primary caregiver. As a parent, it is essential to respond to clingy behaviour with patience and understanding, avoiding frustration or annoyance. The key is to balance comforting the child while gently encouraging independence to foster self-reliance. Offering guidance, reassurance, and praise when the child displays more independent behaviour is essential.

Let me illustrate this with an example. My son was extremely clingy to me, to the extent that I could not even use the washroom for hours. I had to wait for him to sleep before I could carry out any other activities.

When I enrolled him in play school, it was a daunting task as he cried for a month and was reluctant to attend school. Although it was a challenging phase, I kept my hopes high and remained patient, knowing that it would pass. I talked to him about his fears and cleared his misconceptions, assuring him that I was around to protect him even when I was not physically present.

I needed to make him feel secure and safe, so I made sure he could see me from wherever he was present. In exchange for allowing me to carry out my chores, I promised to play his favourite game with him. I kept talking with him from a distance to make him feel comfortable and secure. Gradually, he got used to this idea, which gave me the confidence to take him out to social gatherings.

However, during social gatherings, he would not let me sit anywhere and would start crying if we went to unfamiliar settings. To prepare him for such situations, I started talking to him in advance, explaining what to expect and how to behave. When he started school, I stayed with him for the first month. During the first week, I was with him all the time, while in the second week, I sat near the door and watched him. By the third week, I told him he could not come to me, or else I would not be allowed to stay inside the school. I introduced him to his class teacher as my backup, and he started going to her while keeping an eye on me. In the fourth week, I told him he could not see me, but I was still inside and would be there for him whenever he needed me. Though it was difficult, he agreed to it, and slowly he got used to the idea of me not being around.

However, once a week, he would burst into tears to see if I was around, and I would come to his rescue, assuring him that I was with him. It took five months for him to settle down completely without asking for me. During these five months, I waited outside his school every day for two hours. It was not an easy phase, but I remained patient, consistent, and calm, which helped me pass through it with ease. The two hours that I spent waiting for him became my time to relax, enjoy a walk by the sea, have a cup of coffee, make new friends, and pursue my hobbies. These two hours gave me the energy to carry out my tasks for the rest of the day.

In conclusion, motherhood is not easy, but with patience, consistency, and calmness, we can overcome every challenge that comes our way. Remember, hope is your strength, so never give up.

"Supporting Your Child with ADHD in Navigating Social Challenges: Strategies and Tips"

ADHD can impact various aspects of a child's life, including their social interactions. While not all children with ADHD are introverted, some may exhibit introverted tendencies, finding socializing challenging for a variety of reasons.

Children with ADHD may become easily overwhelmed in social situations, where stimuli can be intense and unpredictable.

The fear of negative social experiences or being judged can contribute to a child with ADHD becoming introverted, as they may prefer the perceived safety of solitude.

Challenges in picking up on social cues and maintaining focus in conversations can make socializing more demanding for children with ADHD.

Recognize and empathize with the challenges your child faces. Understanding their perspective is crucial for effective support.

Create structured social opportunities that allow the child to engage with others in a controlled and predictable environment. For example, plan a play date with a few selected friends at your house as it is a known and comfortable environment. Once the child starts getting comfortable you can plan play dates outside the house.

Work on enhancing social skills through activities that focus on communication, sharing, and understanding others' perspectives.

Facilitate positive interactions with supportive peers who may share common interests or understand the challenges associated with ADHD.

Celebrate and reinforce positive social behaviours. Praise efforts to engage with others, even small steps, to boost their confidence.

Equip your child with strategies to manage overstimulation or anxiety in social settings, such as taking short breaks or finding a quiet space when needed.

Encourage participation in activities aligned with their interests. Shared hobbies can serve as a natural bridge for social connections. For any classes that your child likes, for example, music, art, etc. make sure it's a small group, large groups might make the child feel uncomfortable.

While ADHD may present social challenges, it's essential to focus on the strengths and potential of each child. By understanding their needs, providing appropriate support, and fostering a positive and inclusive environment, we can help these children build meaningful connections and navigate the social landscape more confidently.

"Sleep Solutions for ADHD Kids: Navigating Nighttime Challenges with Ease"

It is not uncommon for children with ADHD to experience sleep-related difficulties that can be attributed to a variety of factors. One of the primary reasons is that ADHD children may have an internal body clock that is delayed, making it difficult for them to fall asleep at conventional bedtime hours. Additionally, hyperactivity, a common symptom of ADHD, can disrupt the ability to wind down and relax at bedtime, while stimulant medications, often prescribed to treat ADHD, may also interfere with sleep patterns.

Moreover, children with ADHD may experience sensory processing issues, which can make them more sensitive to environmental stimuli, thereby making it harder for them to settle down and fall asleep. The inherent difficulty in managing emotions and stimuli can also lead to anxiety or overstimulation, making it even harder for them to relax and fall asleep. Overall, these factors can combine to create a challenging environment for children with ADHD, and it is essential to address their sleep-related issues to ensure that they get the rest they need to function at their best.

My son had terrible sleep patterns. And I was exhausted to the extent that I developed migraines. I had to be injected to sleep once and I was on sleeping pills for a month because my condition had worsened. It is not easy to stay awake all night and then deal with so much of the energy of your child in the day. It's physically, mentally and emotionally exhausting. I don't know how I survived. During those times I could not see any positive ray, I felt I would not be able to keep moving that way, but I survived. Today my son sleeps by 9:30 and wakes up at 7. Although it is not a peaceful sleep. He still wakes up at night, he needs someone's hand to hold due to insecurity, and he still gets restless due to hyperactivity, but he manages and sleeps by himself. So, if any of you are going through this phase, please remember and trust me, this too shall pass.

Let me guide you on how to sail through this.

Establish a calming bedtime routine that begins at the same time every night. Activities such as reading, dimming lights, or taking a warm bath can signal the body that it's time to wind down. I used to give calming massages on his legs and feet.

It is important to avoid giving caffeinated drinks or foods close to bedtime as they can interfere with the sleep pattern. It is recommended to ensure medications are timed appropriately to minimize their impact on sleep. In my case, I have agreed with my son that he should not consume any sugar or junk food after 5 in the evening. I have explained to him that this will help him sleep better at night. Even if he goes to parties, I have made sure that he does not consume any unhealthy food. I have never introduced aerated drinks to him. He has not tasted coffee or aerated drinks till today. Instead, I make fresh juice at home.

To make the bedroom conducive to sleep, it is important to have comfortable bedding, dim lighting, and a noise-free atmosphere. This can help the child relax and fall asleep easily. It is also recommended to reduce exposure to screens (TV, computer, tablets) at least an hour before bedtime. The blue light emitted by screens can interfere with the body's production of melatonin, a hormone that regulates sleep.

Encouraging regular exercise earlier in the day can help release excess energy and promote better sleep. In my case, I make sure to take my son to play in the playground every day in the evening. He runs, jumps, and enjoys using up his energy. It helps him to sleep better at night.

To help calm the mind and body before bedtime, it is important to teach relaxation techniques like deep breathing or progressive muscle relaxation. I have made my son do deep breathing and chant religious mantras to make him sleep peacefully. I also make sure to discuss and talk about positive things that happened in the day. With ADHD, kids tend to think about everything that happens during the day in sleep. Therefore, good thoughts help to have good sleep.

Sleep problems in children with ADHD can significantly impact their daily functioning. By implementing these strategies and seeking professional guidance when needed, parents can help their children develop healthier sleep habits. This can lead to improved overall well-being and better management of ADHD symptoms.

"Effective Ways to Manage Your Child's Anger Issues: Tips for Parents"

In today's world, it is common to observe children exhibiting anger issues, which can be quite a daunting task for parents to comprehend and manage. Often, parents tend to lose their temper and shout at their kids, which only results in reciprocation of the same behaviour from the child. It is important to realize that shouting at your child to control their anger issues is not an effective way to manage their emotions. Instead, it is crucial to first understand and manage your own emotions before helping your child navigate theirs.

Anger is often an outburst of unresolved emotions, and it is important to identify and resolve them. For instance, if you tell your child to go to bed on time to ensure they get a good night's sleep, but they don't listen despite repeated instructions, it is natural to feel angry and worried about their well-being. However, shouting at them won't help them understand your concern, and it may lead to resentment. Instead, it is important to communicate with your child and help them understand why it is important to go to bed on time.

By holding your child and explaining the situation to them, you can help them understand that you are worried about their sleep and well-being. This will create a bond of trust and understanding between you and your child, which will lead to more effective communication and problem-solving in the future. When you use communication to solve problems, you are not only managing your emotions but also teaching your child to use their words and communicate effectively.

It is crucial to make your child realize that feeling upset or angry is normal, but communicating well is essential. By practicing good communication, you can create a positive environment for your child to grow and learn. Whenever your child shouts or displays aggressive behaviour, it is important to remind them that talking and solving problems through communication is far more effective than shouting and yelling.

"Effective Strategies for Teaching Kids to Manage Anger and Avoid Hitting"

Children with ADHD may find it difficult to control their impulses, which can lead to physical reactions like hitting. They may struggle with managing their emotions, and hitting can be a way for them to express themselves when they are feeling overwhelmed or upset.

Dealing with hitting behaviour in children requires a compassionate yet firm approach.

Respond to hitting behaviour calmly but firmly. Explain that hitting is not acceptable and set clear consequences. Use simple language suitable for the child's age to help them understand that hitting hurts people and it's not okay to hurt others. Encourage empathy by asking the child how they would feel in the other person's shoes. Help them understand the impact of their actions on others.

Consider these alternative approaches:

- **Time-outs:** Implement a brief time-out to allow the child to calm down and reflect on their behaviour. This offers a chance for them to understand that hitting results in a pause in activities they enjoy.

Instead of blaming them for how they feel or asking them to take time out as punishment, explain that we should take time out whenever we are angry. This helps us think more rationally and behave appropriately. You can even make it more fun for them by creating a thinking hat or calming hat that they can wear when they are angry. You could also create a calming corner in a room where they can sit and take time out when angry. For instance, you can put their favourite book, soft toy, fidget spinner, and a pillow in the corner. I have created a corner in my child's room, which he always goes to when he is upset or angry. He relaxes in his favourite corner and comes out with a better understanding of his emotions and actions.

- **Loss of privilege:** Temporarily take away a privilege, such as a screen time or a favourite toy, to emphasize the consequences of hitting. Explain that hitting leads to losing the opportunity to enjoy certain activities or items. There are times when talking or time-out does not help. The behaviour is not acceptable or too violent. In such situations, it is important to take action to make children understand the consequences of their actions. It is also important to convey this message to your child that because their actions lead to unwanted or unacceptable consequences, the privilege is taken away temporarily, so they can get time to sit and reflect on their actions.

- **Restitution and repair:** Encourage the child to make amends for their behaviour by apologizing or performing a helpful action for the person they hit. This helps them understand the impact of their actions and fosters empathy. Once your child has realized their mistake, teach them how to make up for their mistakes. The child should know that people and relations should never be taken for granted, and they should respect others' feelings and emotions.

- **Positive reinforcement of good behaviour:** Praise and reward the child when they handle conflicts peacefully or express their feelings without resorting to hitting. Always appreciate your child verbally and let them know how proud you are and how proud they should be for the right actions they have taken. Be specific in your words. For example, "You were upset about your friend teasing you, I could see it was making you angry. But I'm so glad that you took your time out and responded with words and explained to him that you are not liking his behaviour." If you did not allow your child screen time the previous day because of their anger and misbehaviour, allow them an extra 10 minutes of screen or playtime when they show appropriate ways of dealing with anger. Positive reinforcement encourages them to choose more appropriate behaviours.

- **Teaching alternative strategies:** Guide the child in learning better ways to express their emotions, such as using words to communicate feelings or asking for help when upset. Provide them with tools to manage their emotions effectively. If you feel your child has a lot of impulsivity and only words cannot help, ask them to channel their energy positively. Hitting a pillow, using a stress ball, or sensory bottle, kneading clay, tearing paper, scribbling or drawing, bouncing a ball, exercising, dancing, or painting.

- **Model positive behaviour:** Show your child healthy ways to deal with frustration or anger. Role-play situations where you demonstrate calm problem-solving techniques. Children are our reflection. So, they reflect what they see in us. It does not make sense when we shout at our children asking them not to shout or hit them and tell them hitting is not right. Only when we practice healthy ways of addressing our anger, our kids will learn to express them too.

Chapter 26

"Fun and Easy Ways to Help Your Child Discover Their Passion"

Encouraging an ADHD child to explore their interests and choose a suitable hobby can be a challenging task that requires creativity, patience, and a supportive approach. Here are some strategies that can help you in this process:

- **Exposure to different activities:** Encourage your child to try different activities that align with their interests. Take them to a range of places or events related to various hobbies such as sports, art classes, music lessons, nature walks, science experiments, and more. Discuss and explore different options with them, and help them understand the benefits of each activity.

- **Identify their preferences:** Pay attention to what excites your child, and encourage them to explore in that direction. Observe their natural curiosity and enthusiasm for specific activities or topics. Once you identify their preferences, tailor activities or hobbies to suit their interests. For instance, if your child loves movement, consider sports or dance classes. If they enjoy creating things, art or crafting might be appealing.

- **Lead by example:** Children often learn by observing their parents or caregivers. Engage in hobbies yourself or involve other family members in hobbies. This will expose your child to different types of activities and help them find their interests. You can also share your experiences with your child and explain how your hobbies have helped you in life.

- **Start with shorter activities or projects:** ADHD children might struggle with sustained attention, so it's essential to break down hobbies into manageable parts to prevent overwhelm and maintain interest. Don't pay for classes for a long period at once. Let your child take trial classes so that they can decide if they enjoy the activity or not.

- **Celebrate their efforts and successes:** Encourage your child to try new things, and celebrate their efforts and successes. Offer praise and encouragement to motivate them to continue exploring their interests. Show your child what benefits they gain by performing a particular art or taking up a sport.

- **Capitalize on their strengths and abilities:** Identify your child's strengths and abilities and encourage hobbies that align with those strengths. Be patient and flexible; it might take time for your child to find a hobby they truly enjoy. Allow them space to change their minds and explore different options.

- **Consider structured activities:** Sometimes, structured activities with clear instructions and routines can be beneficial for ADHD children. Activities like yoga, karate, gymnastics, and swimming are good for maintaining discipline and help a child focus on instructions. Try to enroll your child in such classes where his overall development is taken care of.

Remember, the goal is not to force your child into a specific hobby but to encourage exploration and enjoyment. Creating a supportive environment where your child feels encouraged to explore their interests at their own pace is key. Avoid comparing your child's progress with others and let them learn and explore in their way. With your support and guidance, they will find their interests and hobbies that will help them grow and thrive.

Chapter 27

"The Power of Gratitude: How Expressing Thanks Can Improve Your Life"

Children with ADHD often face challenges in their daily lives, which can make them feel unlucky or inferior. It is important to help them understand the concept of gratitude and encourage them to count their blessings. A positive attitude can help them regulate their emotions better.

- **Model Gratitude:** Lead by example. Express your gratitude regularly. Share moments when you feel thankful and explain why. Children learn a lot through observation. During dinner time, our family has a routine of sharing our day's experiences. We share what we are happy and grateful for, and even what went wrong, but we try to see the good in it and learn from it. Then, we encourage our kids to reflect on their day and share what they were grateful for. We help them see the positive in any situation they feel went wrong. When you practice this daily, kids form a habit and gain wisdom to see the positive and be grateful in every situation.

- **Gratitude Journal:** Encourage them to keep a gratitude journal. It doesn't have to be lengthy. Start small by asking them to write or draw one thing they are thankful for each day. Make it a routine before bedtime or during family time. There are times when kids don't want to share some things, and it's completely normal. Or maybe some days you are not able to discuss your day with each other. During such times, a gratitude journal helps the child to reflect on their thoughts. My kids have a journal where they don't write every day. They write only things that made a big difference to them in some way.

- **Gratitude Activities:** If writing journals sounds boring to your child, you can make it fun through activities and games. Engage in activities that highlight gratitude, such as making a gratitude jar. Decorate a jar and fill it with notes about things they are grateful for. Then, read these notes together regularly or on weekends or bad days as a reminder to be grateful for the good that happened in the past. You can even play a gratitude game occasionally where every individual will say why they are grateful for every family member in life. This way, you learn to appreciate each other in life and value each other's presence.

- **Volunteering and Helping Others:** Engaging in acts of kindness can instil gratitude. Encourage them to participate in activities that help others, whether it's volunteering at a shelter, helping a neighbour, or simply being kind to classmates. Gratitude should not only be taught in the house but also practiced outside. Teach your kids to be thankful to every individual that helps them in the day. I always say thank you to every taxi driver for giving us a ride. Although we pay them, I still thank them. Now my kids do the same. I say thank you to my house help every day when they leave, for helping me with my household chores, and my kids follow the same. They have learned to say thank you to every person, whether it's a waiter or a watchman. They have learned to be respectful and appreciate everyone around them. This reflects lots of positivity in them. When they show respect to others, others treat them with love and respect. So much love and gratitude help them to be positive and happy in life.

- **Positive Reinforcement:** Acknowledge and praise them when they express gratitude. Positive reinforcement encourages continued practice. So, whenever they help others or use kind words, tell them how they made the other person feel or how the person was happy. Don't praise them by just saying, "I am proud of you." When you involve yourself in their act, it becomes about you, and it makes them liable to make you proud. You have to make them understand that they are doing this for themselves and others, to make someone else's day better. And how their blessings will help them in life. Make sure it's not always about you or making you happy.

- **Visual Aids:** Use visual aids like gratitude charts or boards with pictures or drawings representing things they are thankful for. This makes the concept more tangible and accessible. You can make gratitude cards occasionally. There are mandala prints on gratitude available. The more they see it, it works as a reminder. Utilize books, movies, or shows that emphasize gratitude.

- **Mindfulness and Relaxation Techniques:** Incorporate mindfulness exercises or relaxation techniques to help them appreciate the present moment. Help them understand to be aware and grateful for the life they have, the food they eat, the education they receive, their friends, clothes, toys, everything that they have while many don't. Practices like deep breathing or guided imagery can encourage a sense of gratitude.

By integrating these activities and approaches into their daily lives, ADHD children can gradually develop an understanding of gratitude. Remember, the goal is to make practicing gratitude an enjoyable and integrated part of their routine rather than a chore. So, it is okay if they forget or struggle with gratitude at times. Encourage them gently without pressure. Consistency and patience are key.

"As this Chapter concludes, it's vital to acknowledge that managing behaviour in children with ADHD is an ever-evolving journey. The strategies outlined here serve as guiding lights, but each child is unique, and the path to understanding and supporting them continues. Remember, patience, flexibility, and empathy remain the cornerstones in this ongoing quest. As we move forward, let us carry the lessons learned, adapting and refining our approaches, ensuring that every child's journey is met with understanding, encouragement, and unwavering support."

Conclusion: Embracing the ADHD Journey

As the final pages of this book turn, I stand at the crossroads of reflection and anticipation. This journey, woven with anecdotes, insights, and shared experiences, has been a testament to the resilience, love, and unwavering dedication of parents, caregivers, educators, and the incredible children who navigate the labyrinth of ADHD.

But this isn't just an end; it's a new beginning. Armed with knowledge, empathy, and a deeper understanding, we're poised to redefine the narrative surrounding ADHD. It's not merely a disorder but a unique way of experiencing the world—a tapestry of vibrant colours and unbridled energy.

For every parent who's felt the weight of uncertainty, I hope this book serves as a beacon—a reminder that you're not alone. Your journey, like mine, is a testament to unwavering determination and unconditional love.

To the children with ADHD, you are not defined by this diagnosis. You're a constellation of brilliance, creativity, and boundless potential. Embrace your quirks, cherish your unique perspective, and let the world marvel at the incredible individual you are.

As we bid adieu to these pages, let's carry forth the spirit of understanding and advocacy. Let's challenge stigmas, promote inclusivity, and create spaces where every child, irrespective of their neurological makeup, thrives.

Remember, managing ADHD isn't about erasing differences; it's about celebrating them. It's about creating environments that embrace diversity of thought, learning, and expression.

My deepest gratitude goes to every reader who embarked on this journey. Your willingness to learn, understand, and support is a testament to the change we can collectively bring about in the world.

So, as we part ways, let's carry forward the lessons learned, the empathy gained, and the connections forged. Let's create a world where every child's potential shines brightly, unencumbered by stereotypes or limitations.

Thank you for walking alongside me on this poignant journey. Here's to a future where ADHD isn't a hurdle but a springboard to boundless possibilities.

With warmth and hope,
Sakina Kagalwala.

Testimonials

"Having read only the first four chapters of this book, I can safely say that this particular book can be judged by its cover, or more accurately, its first few pages. I do believe 'Wired for Brilliance' is a brilliant testimony of a mother's tryst, with her child's struggles, as he tries to find his feet, growing up. Every parent in similar situations, and even those who may not be, would find immense value in what lies between the pages of this book. Sakina's endeavor in supporting her son, as she tirelessly marches on, learning, equipping, reflecting, and questioning, are indications of her own growth and evolution as a human being. There's much to be absorbed from this book, which also gives detailed research-backed content, on everything a parent needs to know about ADHD. However, there's one thing that gives it an edge over other such works - it is heartfelt!

I wish Sakina, her son, and her family, All the Very Best!"

Gauri Row Kavi,

Psychologist - Therapist - Coach – Facilitator.

Founder - Self Align.

"Dear Sakina,

I am thrilled to share my heartfelt testimonial for the outstanding book, "Wired for Brilliance". Sakina Kagalwala has been a true beacon of support and understanding for individuals navigating the complex landscape of ADHD. As someone who has personally grappled with the challenges of Attention Deficit Hyperactivity Disorder, finding a compassionate and knowledgeable guide in Sakina's literature will be a meaningful read to all.

One of the most striking aspects of Sakina's approach is the holistic perspective on ADHD. Rather than focusing solely on the challenges, she has skillfully laid out the coping mechanisms through an empowering approach. This will help shift several mindsets from a deficit-based perspective to one that acknowledges the incredible talents and capabilities associated with ADHD.

I wholeheartedly recommend Sakina's book to anyone seeking guidance on their ADHD journey."

Aksheeta Selarka Parikh,
Founder - Casa Vista Montessori Preschool.
Author - My Neighbour's Cat.
Parent to a toddler.

"Right from the Horse's mouth, this book covers most of the management aspects of ADHD from a caregiver's perspective. For someone close who has been having issues and has been evaluated for ADHD, this guide is practically helpful. People struggle with how to connect with and help such a child with ADHD & learning issues, this book eases out most of the problems. After reading the book, I found that a lot of the methods that the author had in place are what we practically recommend to the caregivers, so that was good. This book will clear up a lot of things such as the fact that children with ADHD have brains that are physically different from other children, and how much the criticism received from parents/teachers/classmates can affect them. How can you be fortunate to find a teacher who would be willing to work with children and parents, along with a speech and OT therapist who can help significantly too, etc. It will also ease your mind significantly about medication and clear up a lot of misconceptions you might have. So please be positive in dealing with such special children in the right way. All the best to the author and readers. God Bless."

Dr. Sahir Jamati,
Consulting Psychologist & Psychotherapist.